THE BOOK OF THE INTERNATIONAL

FILM POSTER

THE BOOK OF THE INTERNATIONAL
FILM POSTER

GREGORY J EDWARDS

TIGER BOOKS INTERNATIONAL
LONDON

This edition published in 1988 by
Tiger Books International Ltd.,
London

ISBN 1 870461 61 4

Produced by Grub Street,
Golden House, 28-31 Great
Pulteney Street, London W1R 3DD

First published in Great Britain
by Columbus Books

Printed in Singapore by
Colourwork Press Pte.Ltd.

Contents

7 Introduction

9 Preface
ORIGINS OF THE POSTER A BRIEF SURVEY

13 **1 THE MULTIPLE IMAGE** THE POSTER AND EARLY CINEMA

23 **2 GERMAN POST-WAR ANGST** FROM EXPRESSIONISM TO NEW REALISM

39 **3 CONSTRUCTIVISM AND MONTAGE** TOOLS OF THE RUSSIAN REVOLUTIONARY ARTISTS

55 **4 THE HOLLYWOOD DREAM MACHINE** THE ZENITH OF COMMERCIALISM

105 **5 POSTERS GALORE!** EALING STUDIOS AND THE PURSUIT OF EXCELLENCE

131 **6 THE SPIRIT OF INDEPENDENCE** THE ARTIST AS AUTEUR

159 **7 ART AND LIBERATION** REALISM AND ROMANTICISM IN POLAND AND ITALY

193 **8 COMMITMENT AND ALIENATION** THE POWER OF THE IMAGE

213 **9 NEW DIRECTIONS** DIVERSITY AND COLLECTABILITY

220 Bibliography

222 Index

Acknowledgements

The author particularly wishes to thank
Eric Pulford and Peter Lee of
W. E. Berry.

Photographs

British Institute for
Sugata Sanshiro
Ikimono No Kiroku
Ukigumo

Union Centrale des Arts Decoratifs,
Musée de la Publicité for
Cinématographe Lumière (Auzolle)
Le Biophonographe
Cinématographe Perfectionné
Projections, Animées

Atmosphere for
Tous y Menent leurs Enfants
Les Enfants du Paradis (Lancy)
Les Visiteurs du Soir
Fanny
French Cancan
César
Mon Oncle
Journal d'un curé de campagne
Verdun . . .
Un Vrai Bandit
Le Testament d'Orphée
La Bête Humaine
Maciste contre tous
La Kermesse rouge
Napoléon
Sortilèges
Le Schpountz
Marius
Les Maudits

Ciné-Images for
14 Juillet
Les Enfants du Paradis (Bonneaud)

Other photographs from the author's
collection

The author and publishers also wish to
thank George Allen & Unwin for
permission to quote from J. Leyda,
Kino (p 17–18 , 42) and Thames and
Hudson Ltd for permission to quote
from John Barnicoat, *A Concise
History of Posters* (p 11, 196). The
quotation on p 23, from *A Dictionary of
Arts and Artists* © Peter and Linda
Murray 1959, 1960, 1965, 1968, 1972,
1976, 1983, is reprinted by permission
of Penguin Books Ltd.

Introduction

Until recently, the cinema poster has been viewed by producers and public alike almost exclusively as a selling tool, advertising the claims of the latest film attractions as widely as possible. Ironically, as the mass appeal of the cinema has appeared to decline, posters from an earlier era are increasingly in demand by some collectors as serious works of art.

Among the satisfactions of collecting is the infinite variety of posters produced since the birth of the cinema, from those hastily 'designed' at the printers for some of the less spectacular Hollywood productions to those painted and drawn by the foremost artists of the day, as was particularly the case in France. Yet others reflect current movements in art (such as Expressionism and Constructivism) while some, as studio policy, were produced to the highest possible standards throughout, as at Ealing. There are posters, too, which reflect the strength of a political stance and incorporate the vigour of a revolutionary approach, as in the new Cuban cinema.

The posters reproduced here reflect this variety. Although of necessity an idiosyncratic selection, it has been chosen to illustrate specific contributions to the development of the cinema poster. Some posters remain enjoyable ephemera; some can be appreciated for their nostalgic appeal alone; a few only can claim to be of first-rate design that will stand scrutiny beside the best in the whole range of poster art.

Gregory J. Edwards 1985

The illustrations in this book are not reproduced to scale; original dimensions are given (where available) with the captions, first in inches and then in centimetres. Likewise, designers are named and dates of original production given where known. Page number references in the text margin guide the reader to the appropriate illustration.

Preface
ORIGINS OF THE POSTER A BRIEF SURVEY

The art of poster advertising can be traced back to the ancient Egyptians, who understood the advantages of mural advertisements, and to ancient Athens and Rome where booksellers advertised their latest productions on their shop walls. The dictionary defines the word 'poster' as a large printed bill or placard for posting. The first printed bill in England was produced by William Caxton in 1477 and until the end of the 18th century all printed bills were purely typographical with the occasional crude woodcut motif. These printed bills, used for official proclamations and advertisements for meetings and theatres, were displayed on walls, hoardings and posts. In 1579 John Northbrooke remarked:

> 'They used to set up their bills upon posts some certain days before, to admonish people to make resort to their theatres.'

Even the plays of the time made frequent reference to the posting of playbills. For instance in the play *A Warning to Fair Women* of 1599, Tragedy accuses Comedy, declaring:

> 'Tis you have kept this theatre so long
> Painted in playbills upon every post.'

With the Industrial Revolution came the further requirement of advertising for the cumulative number of goods being made available to the public. The invention of lithography by Alois Senefelder of Austria in 1798 resulted in a cheaper and faster method of producing posters to advertise these products. The basis of lithography is that water will not adhere to a greasy surface. The artist's design is drawn or painted directly onto a thick slab of stone with a greasy chalk or ink. The stone is then wetted so that when the greasy poster ink is applied it will only adhere to the already greasy areas. The image can then be printed directly onto paper.

Francisco Goya began to use this new technique from 1819 to produce bull-fighting scenes, and from 1820 to 1822 Théodore Géricault produced lithographs of horses and scenes of poverty observed in the streets of London. Honoré Daumier used the process to great advantage from the 1830s to produce over 4000 bitterly satirical, political caricatures. Enlarged book illustrations began to appear in shop windows to publicize new books from the 1830s, including Raffet's advertisements for Norvin's *History of Napoleon* and Johannot's for *Don Quichotte* in 1845. In 1868 Edouard Manet produced *Les Chats*, a printed notice for the J. Rothschild publishing house, which had a central lithographic drawing of two cats on a rooftop, though the image was still secondary to the printed word. From 1859 to 1866 Jules Chéret, who was born in 1836, the same year that Brisset invented the rotary lithographic press, was perfecting his typographic and chromolithographic techniques in London and producing posters for books, operas and music halls. Returning to Paris in 1866 he began producing colour lithographic posters from his own press. He perfected a style that succeeded in marrying text and image, creating a uniform composition. The poster lettering was left to his friend Madaré, thereby displaying an indifference to advertising which reinforces the theory that Chéret was at heart a mural painter who used the street to exhibit his work.

Roger Marx, an influential art critic of the time, describes the effect caused by this colourful intrusion into workaday life where:

'. . . . streets themselves conspire against the relaxation of the eye, the mind; the ever changing decor which covers the city's walls forcefully draws our attention, and even the busiest, most sceptical passer-by must submit to the charm of the sight that has been flung into his path, follow the spirited arabesque of the design, delight in the variegated flora blooming among the grey stones. The fact is, that to be sure to make an impression and better to convince, Advertising has called upon Art for help; it has borrowed the poetry of allegories, it has become image and its beautiful appearance has bestowed upon it, with unexpected efficiency, the indefeasible right to the aesthete's attention.'

The subjects of Chéret's posters are based in popular folk art: frivolous dancing figures from music halls, circuses, cabarets, pantomimes and grand and comic operas prevail. Henri de Toulouse-Lautrec used the same subjects but went one stage further. He used the poster to express his own experiences and therefore his illustrations tend to be more descriptive and devoid of the traditional elements found in Chéret's work. Lautrec's satirical posters were not, however, as popular with the public, or the patrons, as were Chéret's. One can imagine the response to his poster for the *Divan Japonais* where the star of the show, Yvette Guilbert, is placed at the edge of the poster, headless, whilst Lautrec's friend Jane Avril is the dominant figure of the design. Lautrec's posters, limited in number as they are (31 compared to more than 1000 by Chéret) are nonetheless a major contribution to the development of the genre.

ART NOUVEAU AND AFTER

Most countries were by now producing posters. In Vienna the Secessionists Gustav Klimt, Koloman Moser, Josef Hoffmann and Alfred Roller were producing posters similar to those of Charles Rennie Mackintosh and his colleagues at the Glasgow School of Art. These were all in the Art Nouveau style which in France, apart from Toulouse-Lautrec, was dominated by the extraordinary work of Alphonse Mucha. His posters of Sarah Bernhardt, using the classic iconography of swirling hair, sumptuous costumes, ornate mosaics and exotic vegetation, are now his most famous. Bernhardt commissioned Mucha in 1894 to design the poster for *Gismonda* which became his first important work. Other poster artists working in the Art Nouveau style were Leopoldo Metlicovitz, G. M. Mataloni and Alfred Hohenstein in Italy and Will Bradley and Edward Penfield in the United States. How posters were developing in

America can be gauged by the impressions of an English visitor, the poster designer F. Scotson-Clark, in the 1890s.

'Until the winter of 1894, the artistic poster was practically unknown in the United States. The only things of the kind, and they were very excellent and very original, were the *Harper's* magazine window bills by Edward Penfield. But during the latter part of 1893 and the early half of 1894, the name and work of Aubrey Beardsley had become known, and popular as was his success amongst a large class in England, his fame was tenfold in America. Every twopenny-halfpenny town had its 'Beardsley Artist', and large cities simply teemed with them. Some borrowed his ideas and adapted them to their own uses; others imitated, until one asked oneself: 'is this done by the English or American B?'.

The American B was Scotson-Clark's nickname for Will Bradley.

James Pryde, who had studied in Paris, felt that with few exceptions English posters were anything but striking.

'Poster art in England was just being redeemed by Dudley Hardy whose *Yellow Girl* for the Gaiety Theatre was a clever piece of work; Maurice Greiffenhagen, later a Royal Academician, who did a poster for the *Pall Mall Budget* and Frederick Walker whose *Woman in White* (1871) really seemed like an enlarged reproduction of a black-and-white drawing of his own. There was also Aubrey Beardsley's poster for what was then regarded as the advanced theatre in London, the Avenue (1894). This last found little favour with *Punch* which, referring to it, made the suggestion: 'ave a new poster. There were oases in the desert of others designed by regular workers for various firms. This was the condition of affairs when I decided to become a poster artist.'

This condition resulted in Pryde reacting against the use of lithography to produce hand printed posters in relatively small runs with the use of stencils. He joined forces with William Nicholson, a fellow student from Paris, and under the name 'Beggarstaff Brothers' they produced some extremely original posters.

Interest in the poster was phenomenal and some printers even produced smaller versions of their better posters for the now-avid collector who otherwise was not averse to peeling his favourite poster from the wall. Articles, magazines and books about posters proliferated. In France there were *La Plume, La Critique, L'Estampe et l'Affiche* (*l'estampe* was a poster deprived of its advertising element), *L'Image, Les Affiches illustrées, Les Affiches étrangères, L'Affiche Belge* and *Les Maîtres de l'Affiche*. In the United States appeared: *Scribners, The Bill Poster, Poster Lore, Posters in Miniature* and *The Modern Poster* (a collection of *Scribner* articles). In England there were *The Studio, The Poster Magazine* and *The Illustrated Poster* and in Belgium *L' Affiche artistique*. Not surprisingly then, in 1897 the *Revue des Deux Mondes* defined the period as 'The Age of the Poster'.

1 THE MULTIPLE IMAGE THE POSTER AND EARLY CINEMA

The cinema was born in the 'Age of the Poster', which was now employed to advertise this new form of cheap entertainment, aimed generally at the working classes. Cheap entertainment so far included the music hall, the popular theatre, carnivals and the circus. Music hall and theatre posters stayed on display for as long as the performers, or performances, remained successful, or until the termination of a contracted period. Circus posters, however, were transient, as the very nature of the circus demanded a regular change of venue, sometimes daily.

In the United States, circus posters were despatched to the site by rail, well in advance of the performance. Each poster was made up of individual sheets of around 28″ by 42″. The standard poster used 16 of these sheets and the advance despatch would include anything between 5000 and 8000 of them. They were pasted up on the sides of barns, buildings, and billboards either being constructed by, or rented to, the circus companies. In 1892 the Ringling Brothers Circus used 24,000 sheets for their venue in Topeka, Kansas; in other words, 1500 posters each measuring around 7 feet by 19 feet!

The major circus companies used the more prestigious printing houses, which at that time were: the Strobridge Lithographic Company of Cincinnati, Ohio; Adolph Friedlander of Hamburg, Germany; David Allen and Sons of Belfast and Harrow; and the houses of Charles Levy and Alban Chaix in Paris. In Britain and the United States the smaller circus companies continued to use the older form of letterpress. The quality of printing created by these companies was excellent, with every colour imaginable and each illustrated character presented in infinite detail.

The Chaix Printing Company originally belonged to Jules Chéret, who sold out to Chaix in 1881 but stayed on as director and chief lithographer. It was perhaps providential that the first pre-cinema posters should in fact be designed by this established master. In 1892 he designed the poster for Emile Reynaud's Optical

Pantomimes Lumineuses
Jules Chéret
34½ x 49/88 x 124
1892

The first 'film' poster to be created by a master poster artist represents the projected images of Columbine and *Pauvre Pierrot* animated by Emile Reynaud's Praxinoscope before an audience at the Musée Grévin.

Theatre, entitled *Pantomimes Lumineuses*. The Théâtre Optique was the culmination of developments in producing moving images on a screen. Reynaud's original invention of 1876, the Praxinoscope, presented a series of drawings on a moving strip, with the aid of mirrors set at angles; it was improved ten years later to project images on to a screen before an audience. By the end of 1888 the images were painted directly on to perforated strips of celluloid. These images, about four by five centimetres in size, were drawn in white on a black ground or were colour-tinted. On October 28th 1892 they were presented to a paying audience for the first time, at the Cabinet Fantastique in the Musée Grévin, which was situated in the Boulevard Montmartre in Paris. From the opening till its close in March 1899, 12,800 performances were attended by 500,000 visitors. Over this eight-year period Reynaud produced five films for the programme: *Un Bon Bock* (15 minutes), *Clown et ses Chiens* (10 minutes), *Pauvre Pierrot* (15 minutes), *Un Rêve au Coin du Feu* (12 minutes) and *Autour d'une Cabine* (15 minutes). Chéret's extremely colourful poster depicts the *Pauvre Pierrot* film featuring Pierrot and Columbine. *12*

The novelty of Reynaud's Optical Theatre caught on, and copies and variations appeared, including the Pipon Frères' Cinographoscope of 1896, for which the anonymous *Projections Animées* poster was designed. *19*

In 1894 Thomas Edison demonstrated his Kinetoscope in Paris. This apparatus recorded movement, but was unable to project it, the images being viewed peep-show style. Louis Lumière, who had invented the dry-plate process in 1881, was so impressed by this demonstration that before the year was out he had developed, with his brother Auguste's assistance, the Cinématographe, which was a combination of camera and projector. On December 28th 1895, the Lumière brothers projected some of their films to a paying public at the Grand Café in Paris.

Chéret submitted a poster design to the Lumière brothers, which was apparently rejected. The three existing Lumière posters were designed by Henri Brispot, Abel Truchet and Auzolle. Brispot's poster illustrates an official controlling the crowd queuing to see the show and Truchet's shows an audience startled by the apparent onrush of the Lumières' train in *Arrivée d'un Train en Gare*. Auzolle's poster of 1896 depicts an audience viewing the Lumières' humorous *L'Arroseur Arrosé*. This simple *20* gag shows a gardener hosing his garden, whilst a boy sneaks up behind him and puts his foot on the hose, halting the flow of water. The puzzled gardener looks down the nozzle and gets a soaking when the boy takes his foot away. The poster, with typographical translations, was used world-wide and is considered to be the first poster representing the first fiction film. It illustrates the audience in colour watching black and white images on a screen. This style of poster was used internationally for all variations of the Lumières' Cinématographe and would often show a beam of light, or the projector, so that the public did not mistake the events as being theatrical.

Similar imagery was used in Albert George Morrow's poster, printed by David Allen and Sons, for Edison's life-size Animated Pictures, with the middle-class audience watching a screen where a blank space has been overprinted with the day's attractions at the Curzon Hall, Birmingham. David Allen and Sons, founded in Belfast in 1857, opened another branch in Harrow in 1897. They produced a vast quantity of theatrical and 'show' posters, including all those for the Gilbert and Sullivan operas. Their staff of designers included John Hassall, William True, Alick P. F. Ritchie, Tom Browne and Albert Morrow. Their success was partly due to the complete package offered to their clients: artwork by professional designers; printing facilities; exclusive bill posting locations and a catalogue of stock designs.

STOCK POSTERS AND CREATIVE DESIGNS

Around 1900 in the United States, the American Entertainment Company used a poster portraying the audience of a sumptuous theatre watching a black and white image of a marching band on the screen. The poster was printed by the Donaldson Show Print Company of Cincinnati, which, like Strobridge, had produced thousands of theatrical and 'show' posters. They were also well known for their wide range of stock posters for plays and circuses.

16 The stock poster became popular when the day's attractions were either indicated by, or appeared on a card held by, a beautiful woman. The poster for *Salle de l'Etoile* designed by Louis Coulet in 1902 is a prime example. Chéret had already produced what must have been the first pre-cinema stock poster for the *Projections Artistiques* of 1890, which presents a young woman simply holding a card displaying the show's timetable. Francois Flemeng's poster for the Phono-Cinema-Theatre depicts a woman, casually leaning on a projector, holding a card listing artists who will appear in a selection of '*visions animées*'. The list is headed by Mme Sarah Bernhardt.

Film-makers like the Pathé brothers and Leon Gaumont sought out creative workshops to produce their posters. Candido Aragonese de Faria, already celebrated for his caricatures of the singer Paulus, was the head of his own printing firm which began producing posters almost exclusively for Pathé. Adrien Barrère, who created around 100 posters for Pathé in his individual caricature style, designed

20 the poster *Tous y Mènent leurs Enfants*! in 1908. Once again, in the original the audience is portrayed in colour and the screen image in black and white; in this case, however, all the members of the audience are recognizable heads of state with their children watching a film about themselves. The use of royalty in these early posters was a device to assure the general public of the respectability of the cinematograph.

19 The same device is also evident in the poster for *Le Biophonographe*, which was one of many attempts to produce sound accompaniment to film by the synchronization of a gramophone with a projector. Amongst the audience shown in this poster are King Edward VII, Chamberlain, François-Joseph, Leopold II, Czar Nicolas II and Henri Rochefort. However, the point of emphasizing the respectability of the cinematograph in this poster is somewhat obscured as the majority of the heads of state seem more interested in the young woman to the right of the screen than in the showing of Molière's *Médecin malgré lui*. Another poster for a synchronized show was designed by Tamagno in 1907 for the *Cinématographe and Phonographe*, illustrating, in a style reminiscent of Alphonse Mucha, the audience viewed from behind, looking at a black and white sword-fencing image on a circular screen, once again indicated by a young woman to the left of the screen.

21 The poster illustrated for the *Cinématographe Perfectionné* of 1896 presents the Joly-Normandin system of projection. It was printed by Charles Levy in Paris, who had printed Lautrec's first poster for the Moulin Rouge in 1891. The Joly-Normandin system was used to project, amongst others, the Lumières' *Arrivée d'un Train en gare* and *Arroseur Arrosé*. Unfortunately this system of projection was also associated with the cinema's first tragedy, the Charity Bazaar Fire. The Charity Bazaar was an annual social event in Paris and in 1897 was held near the Champs-Elysées on an open space which had been cleared for building. All the stalls were made of wood and canvas and painted to represent shops and inns of the 16th century. A larger booth was constructed for a cinematograph show, which was to use a projection light source of ether vapour. The show was very popular and attended by many aristocrats with their children. One afternoon the projection lamp went out and was relit too soon, causing a flash of flame which quickly engulfed the flimsy canvas construction; within a matter of minutes over a hundred people had been burned alive.

OUT OF THE SHADOWS

It is difficult in these days of wide screen, technicolor films with stereo sound and spectacular special effects to imagine the impact these early black and white, silent snippets of film had on the general public. Maxim Gorky evokes the magical

Kyrle Picture Palace, Ross
5¹¹⁄₁₆ x 8⅞/14.4 x 22.6

A typical early letterpress cinema bill.

atmosphere created by such a show, experienced when he visited the Lumières' demonstration in Moscow in 1896.

'Last night I was in the Kingdom of Shadows.

If you only knew how strange it is to be there. It is a world without sound, without colour. Everything there – the earth, the trees, the people, the water and the air – is dipped in monotonous grey. Grey rays of the sun across the grey sky, grey eyes in grey faces, and the leaves of the trees are ashen grey. It is not life but its shadow, it is not motion but its soundless spectre.

Here I shall try to explain myself, lest I be suspected of madness or indulgence in symbolism. I was at Aumont's and saw Lumière's cinematograph – moving photography. The extraordinary impression it creates is so unique and complex that I doubt my ability to describe it with all its nuances. However, I shall try to convey its fundamentals.

When the lights go out in the room in which Lumière's invention is shown, there suddenly appears on the screen a large grey picture, 'A Street of Paris' – shadows of a bad engraving. As you gaze at it, you see carriages, buildings and people in various poses, all frozen into immobility. All this is in grey, and the sky above is also grey – you anticipate nothing new in this all too familiar scene, for you have seen pictures of Paris street scenes more than once. But suddenly a strange flicker passes through the screen and the picture stirs to life. Carriages coming from somewhere in the perspective of the picture are moving straight at you, into the darkness in which you sit; somewhere from afar people appear and loom larger as they come closer to you; in the foreground children are playing with a dog, bicyclists tear along, and pedestrians cross the street picking their way among the carriages. All this moves, teems with life and, upon approaching the edge of the screen, vanishes somewhere beyond it.

And all this in strange silence where no rumble of wheels is heard, no sound of footsteps or of speech. Nothing. Not a single note of the intricate symphony that always accompanies the movements of people. Noiselessly, the ashen-grey foliage of the trees sways in the wind, and the grey silhouettes of the people, as though condemned to eternal silence and cruelly punished by being deprived of all the colours of life, glide noiselessly along the grey ground. Their smiles are lifeless, even though their movements are full of living energy and are so swift as to be almost imperceptible. Their laughter is soundless, although you see their muscles contracting in their grey faces. Before you a life is surging, a life deprived of words and shorn of the living spectrum of colours – the grey, the soundless, the bleak and dismal life.

It is terrifying to see, but it is the movement of shadows, only of shadows. Curses and ghosts, the evil spirits that have cast entire cities into eternal sleep, come to mind and you feel as though Merlin's vivious trick is being enacted before you. As though he had bewitched the entire street, he compressed its many-storied buildings from roof-tops to foundations to yard-like size. He dwarfed the people in corresponding proportion, robbing them of the power of speech and scraping together all the pigment of earth and sky into a monotonous grey colour.

Under this guise he shoved his grotesque creation into a niche in the dark room of a restaurant. Suddenly something clicks, everything vanishes and a train appears on the screen. It speeds straight at you – watch out! It seems as though it will plunge into the darkness in which you sit, turning you into a ripped sack full of lacerated flesh and splintered bones, and crushing into dust and into broken fragments this hall and this building, so full of women, wine, music and vice.

Salle de l'Etoile
Louis Coulet
46½ x 62¾/117.7 x 159.4
1902

A fine example of an early 'stock' poster, where space is provided for the imprinting of the day's attractions.

But this, too, is but a train of shadows.

Noiselessly, the locomotive disappears beyond the edge of the screen. The train comes to a stop, and grey figures silently emerge from the cars, soundlessly greet their friends, laugh, walk, run, bustle, and . . . . are gone. And here is another picture. Three men seated at the table, playing cards. Their faces are tense, their hands move swiftly. The cupidity of the players is betrayed by the trembling fingers and by the twitching of their facial muscles. They play . . . . Suddenly, they break into laughter, and the waiter who has stopped at their table with beer, laughs too. They laugh until their sides split but not a sound is heard. It seems as if these people have died and their shadows have been condemned to play cards in silence unto eternity. Another picture. A gardener watering flowers. The light grey stream of water, issuing from a hose, breaks into a fine spray. It falls upon the flowerbeds and upon the grass blades weighted down by the water. A boy enters, steps on the hose, and stops the stream; the gardener stares into the nozzle of the hose, whereupon the boy steps back and a stream of water hits the gardener in the face. You imagine the spray will reach you, and you want to shield yourself. But on the screen the gardener has already begun to chase the rascal all over the garden and having caught him, gives him a beating. But the beating is soundless, nor can you hear the gurgle of the water as it gushes from the hose left lying on the ground.'

It was not long before the 'Kingdom of Shadows' became familiar to many thousands of eager visitors. Soon after the turn of the century regular picture shows were being given in permanent buildings which were called nickelodeons in America and penny gaffs in Britain. As with the circus, performances changed regularly and the theatre fronts were plastered with constantly renewed imagery. However, the venue was now static and its status gradually improving. Poster art in various countries quickly adapted to the demands of the cinema. In Italy, for example, the comic styles of Marchetti and G. Grande were applied to cinema posters, but were overshadowed by Mauzan's designs produced for the Riccordi printing house. These could be comic or highly atmospheric, as in his designs for Gaumont's mystery serials directed by Louis Feuillade. In Hungary the cinema was held in high regard and, unlike other countries, attracted professional actors, in this case from the Budapest National Theatre. The posters here were designed by such renowned artists as Mihaly Biró and Imres Foldes, producing striking imagery for the Apollo and Projectorgraph cinemas many years before the First World War. As the films themselves had grown from single scenes to full-length features, so the posters paralleled their increasing sophistication.

STANDARDIZING SIZES

Soon the exhibitors acquired frames in which to display their posters, so creating a standardization in poster sizes. In the United States the 42″ x 28″ sheet eventually became known as a one-sheet, in the marginally reduced format of 41″ x 27″. (For all the following measurements the first number denotes height, the second, width.) The next size up is a three-sheet, 81″ x 41″. From there on sizes are doubled; a six-sheet is 81″ x 82″; a twelve-sheet 82″ x 162″ and so on. (The smaller American sizes, printed on card, are defined in Chapter 4.) In Britain the single sheet is called a double-crown, measuring 30″ x 20″. Twice this, either 60″ x 20″ or 30″ x 40″ (the now common format), is known as a quad. A four-sheet is 60″ x 40″; a six-sheet can either be vertical, 90″ x 40″, or broadside, 60″ x 60″, and so on. In France the basic sheet size is 80 cm x 60 cm, doubling to 80 cm x 120 cm, then 160 cm x 120 cm (the current standard size), then 160 cm x 240 cm and so on. The multi-sheet billboard poster used for the circus is rarely used for cinema nowadays.

Le Biophonographe
15¾ x 19½/40 x 50
1900

A poster depicting an
audience of notables and
demonstrating one of the
many attempts to
produce synchronized
sound.

**Projections Animées,
Cinographoscope**
47¼ x 63/120 x 160

Illustrated here is the
Pipon Frères'
Cinographoscope,
a projection device which
was also capable of
recording and printing
images on film.

Tous y Mènent leurs Enfants!
Adrien Barrère
47¼ x 63/120 x 160
1908

To assure the public of the respectability of the cinema, posters often depicted audiences of notable figures and heads of state.

Cinématographe Lumière
Auzolle
39½ x 53/100 x 135

The first film poster to depict the first fiction film: the Lumières' *L'Arroseur Arrosé.*

Cinématographe Perfectionné
25½ x 35¾/65 x 91
1896

This poster presents scenes from various films including the Lumières' *Arrivée d'un Train en gare* and *L'Arroseur Arrosé.*

2 GERMAN POST-WAR ANGST FROM EXPRESSIONISM TO NEW REALISM

In their *Dictionary of Art and Artists*, Peter and Linda Murray have described Expressionism as:

'The search for expressiveness of style by means of exaggerations and distortions of line and colour; a deliberate abandon of the naturalism in Impressionism in favour of a simplified style which should carry far greater emotional impact.'

The Expressionist movement had its origins in the German branch of Art Nouveau, called Jugendstil after the magazine *Jugend* which was first published in 1896. The specific characteristic of Jugendstil, particularly in poster design, was the element of fantasy. Out of this fantasy grew an Expressionist style which was peculiarly Germanic or Nordic, further influences of which can be traced in the hysterical paintings of Edvard Munch, particularly *The Cry* of 1895.

Expressionist forms first appeared in the paintings of the Blaue Reiter group, isolated artists such as Kokoschka and Beckmann, and Die Brücke, a group whose wild colours were similar to those employed by the French Fauves. Die Brücke founded a Society of the Friends of the Brücke whose members were amateur engravers and collectors and whose subscriptions to the society necessitated a form of advertising; this was to become the first link between Expressionism and the poster. Ernst Ludwig Kirchner, one of the founders of Die Brücke in 1905, produced a poster for the group in 1910 epitomizing the dramatic tendencies in Expressionist art.

In the cinema, German Expressionism is characterized by a group of films made during the years following the First World War up till the advent of National Socialism. In essence these form a small percentage of the total film output of the time, but are nevertheless the films of major interest, the rest being commercial escapist fare. The average number of films produced each year was around 200, an amount attributable to the injection of capital into cinema made under the auspices of General Ludendorff,

Berlin die Sinfonie Der Grosstadt
1927

Walther Ruttmann's film was influenced by the Kino-Eye principles of the Russian documentary film-maker Dziga Vertov. These principles were echoed in Russian film poster design and elements from them subsequently utilized in this poster.

**Das Cabinet des Dr.
Caligari**
Otto Stahl-Arpke
26¾ x 39¼/68 x 100
1919

A fusion of the arts of
painting, cinema and
poster design resulted in
a superlative
Expressionist film poster.

Faust (*Eine Deutsche
Volkssage*)
Karl Michel
1926

The medieval woodcut
style of this poster
emphasizes the German
legends brought to life in
the film.

Chief of Staff to Field Marshal (later President) Hindenburg. The capital, a third of which came from the government and the rest from industry, launched the giant film company, Ufa (Universum Film Aktien Gesellschaft) in 1917. Ludendorff's idea of government intervention was to match Allied propaganda, which he regarded as highly effective.

The signing of the Armistice in 1918, the resources of Ufa, plus the prevailing mood of intellectual excitement, or *Aufbruch*, resulted in film-makers using the medium of film to present their own form of Expressionism, embodying violent contrasts, chiaroscuro and shadow, their characters bedevilled by fatalism, destiny and doom.

The first key Expressionist film was *The Cabinet of Dr. Caligari*, directed by   *24* Robert Wiene in 1919 for a mere $18,000. Erich Pommer acquired the script from the Austrian writer Carl Mayer and the poet anarchist Hans Janowitz. Their original story is about a young man of unstable mind who is persecuted by his psychiatrist (an intended indictment of all authority). Pommer altered the story so that the now deluded young madman sees the kindly psychiatrist as a homicidal maniac, a fairground showman who uses a somnambulist to commit his murders for him. There were few technical innovations, with a camera which in fact remained static, but an intelligent use of the iris-in/iris-out method for scene changes was employed. The acting by Werner Krauss as the psychiatrist and Conrad Veidt as the corpse-like somnambulist is highly Expressionistic, as are the sets designed by Herman Warm, Walter Rohrig and Walter Reimann, all of whom belonged to the Berlin 'Sturm' group, convinced Expressionists who, in Warm's own words believed that 'films must be drawings brought to life'. The sets, with their deliberately distorted perspective, are in fact three-dimensional drawings, consisting of flat planes covered in curved lines and whorls and all set at acute angles to one another to represent streets, walls and houses. These effects transcribed easily to posters, as can be seen in Otto Stahl-Arpke's poster for this film. It depicts the fairground scene, complete with curiously angled tents, where the bespectacled Caligari invites the public, many of whom are wearing enormous stove-pipe hats, to come and see Cesare the somnambulist.

This film and *The Golem* of 1920 were the major, and only true, Expressionist films of the period, drawing themes, styles and visual motifs directly from the movement. However, certain features of Expressionism in art direction and acting became highlights of the German cinema up till the later 1920s. Paul Wegener's version of *The Golem* was an allegorical story of a man-made giant created by the Rabbi Loew to protect the oppressed Jews of Prague. Wegener had learned the art of dynamic composition and chiaroscuro lighting whilst working in Max Reinhardt's Deutsche Theatre in Berlin. His film is a mixture of dark, oppressive sets and sun-drenched streets, twilight terror and ethereal fantasy. Carl Boese, who shared director billing with Wegener, created all the trick photography on set through double exposure of the negative within the camera. The rich Gothic sets for the medieval ghetto were designed by Hans Poelzig, the leader of German architectural Expressionism, who had worked with Max Reinhardt on stage productions and built the fantastic showplace of the Grosses Schauspielhaus in Berlin.

The anonymous hysterical poster for *The Golem* has overtones of Edvard   *28* Munch, with the ghetto buildings screaming out the title of the film. The Golem actually appears diminutive in this poster, whereas in Theo Matejko's design, which   *29* uses a more graphic style, the Golem towers over the prostrate Rabbi's daughter. Matejko is renowned for the highly effective posters he produced for the Deutsche Demokratische Partie in the 1928 elections.

Another who began his career with Max Reinhardt, as a versatile and popular comedian, was Ernst Lubitsch, already directing films by the end of the war. One of Lubitsch's protogées was the torrid Polish actress Barbara Apollonia Chalupiec, better known as Pola Negri. She starred in his *Carmen* of 1918, which although shot on a small budget, and in the studio, was voted best German film of the year. The poster for *Carmen* was designed by Josef Fenneker, a prolific designer who created many film posters between 1919 and 1924 for the prestigious film theatre the Marmorhaus in Kurfurstendamm. Among those he produced, in a highly Expressionistic style, was a striking poster of Conrad Veidt in Murnau's *Der Januskopf* of 1920, which was based on Stevenson's *Dr Jekyll and Mr Hyde*.

28   Pola Negri, who was outstanding in other Lubitsch costume dramas, most notably *Madame Dubarry* (1919), also made films for other directors, including Paul Ludwig Stein, Dmitri Buchowetski and Georg Jacoby. The poster for Georg Jacoby's *Karussell des Lebens* (*Matrimonial Holiday*) of 1919 is illustrated on page 28 and portrays Negri dancing to the music of a mandolin player. In fact she claimed to have trained as a dancer in St Petersburg before being brought to Berlin by Max Reinhardt. However, the major actress of the German silent cinema was, without doubt, the legendary Asta Nielsen. Born in Copenhagen in 1883, she spent many years on the stage before her engagement with Nordisk films. In 1911 the founder of Ufa, Paul Davidson, lured her to Germany where she later settled with her husband and director, Urban Gad. She was dark haired, with large expressive eyes and an ability to use gestures sparingly, move with grace and to create an intense relationship with the characters she played. She had an eye for physical detail and the use of appropriate dress, which she used to accentuate her slenderness. She rapidly became a superstar and a pin-up actress of the First World War in Germany and France.

31   In 1920, Asta Nielsen formed her own production company, Art Film A. G., to produce a topical version of *Hamlet*. This was the Hamlet of Danish legend, not Shakespearean tragedy, where Hamlet is a princess disguised as a prince in order to inherit the throne of Denmark. This grandiose film was directed by Sven Gade and Heinz Schall and photographed by one of Europe's finest cameramen at that time, Curt Courant. Nielsen commissioned artists to design imaginative posters for her own productions which would probably include the very dramatic poster for *Hamlet*.

32   In 1925 F. W. Murnau directed Emil Jannings, Lil Dagover and Werner Krauss in another classic drama, Molière's *Tartüff*. Murnau's sumptuous adaptation of this satire on hypocrisy in French society became a more elaborate and complex German version. Emil Jannings' acting was highly stylized: dressed entirely in black, he was perpetually reading from a diminutive Bible held close to his face. Murnau concentrated on composition in movement, balancing lighting and space, observing specific objects in detail, like the lace negligé in the bedroom scene, the design of Oregon's ring, the pattern on the counterpane and the porcelain clock. The poster by Theo Matejko illustrates the hypocrite Tartuff lusting after Oregon.

The script for *Tartüff* was by Carl Mayer, who also collaborated with Murnau in experiments to rid the silent film of subtitled dialogue. A classic example of what came to be known as *Kammerspiel* (literally chamber-dramas or intimate screenplays) is *The Last Laugh* (1925), starring Emil Jannings as a proud and resplendently uniformed hotel commissionaire, whose life collapses around him when he is demoted to lavatory attendant. The film uses sparse decor and an intimate psychological content which owes much to the Max Reinhardt school, Murnau's training ground.

Murnau's last film in Germany before leaving for America was *Faust* in 1926. It starred the Swedish actor Gosta Eckman and Emil Jannings, who stole the film with his role as the devil. The original legend became lost in Murnau's graphic assimilation of Hans Kyser's script, which exploited both Marlowe and Goethe and other German folk sagas. The film contained splendid medieval settings designed by Robert Herlth and Walter Rohrig, and brilliant special effects, particularly Mephisto and Faust flying across the world, over model landscapes and towns, photographed by Carl Hoffman

Karussell des Lebens
1919

The poster depicts one of Ernst Lubitsch's protogées, Pola Negri, dancing to the music of a mandolin player.

Der Golem: Wie Er in die Welt Kam
29 x 39¼/74 x 100
1920

The paintings of Edvard Munch had a great influence on the Expressionist movement, most evident in this poster's seething townscape.

Der Golem: Wie Er in die Welt Kam
Theo Matejko
1920

To protect the oppressed Jews of Prague, the Rabbi Loew created the Golem, an animated clay giant who is shown here towering over the Rabbi's daughter.

Hamlet
27 x 37/69 x 94
1920

Asta Nielsen was wholly involved in her films, even to the extent of commissioning film posters. As *Hamlet* was her own production, it is probable that this dramatic poster was authorized by her.

Die Büchse der Pandora
1929

The film's Expressionist atmosphere has become secondary to the provocative presence of Louise Brooks, who dominates this essentially Art Deco poster.

Faust
1926

A more representational image than for the *Faust* on page 25, this poster shows Mephistopheles tantalizing Faust with the mirror image of the beautiful Marguerite.

from a dolly suspended from railway tracks in the ceiling. With the opening shot of the city totally enveloped by the devil's cloak and the scene where Lucifer is expelled from Heaven by a magnificent winged angel, Murnau's *Faust* remains one of the most ingenious films of the silent era. Karl Michel's woodcut-style poster gives emphasis to the folk-tale treatment of the Faustian legend.

25

FUTURE AND PRESENT: TALES OF TWO CITIES

After the 1918 Armistice, Germans became involved not only in the examination of tyranny but also of a life without it. To some the alternative seemed to be anarchist revolution, a concept encapsulated by the 'Novembergruppe', an artistic movement founded by the painter Max Pechstein, formerly a member of Die Brücke. The movement sought a rejection of conventional values with a manifesto represented and counter-signed by delegates of the intellectual and artistic élite of the new Germany, including Karl Schmidt-Rottluff, Erich Heckel, Emil Nolde, Lyonel Feininger, Walter Gropius, Viking Eggeling, Kurt Weill, Bertolt Brecht and Paul Hindemith, among others. The films produced between 1920 and 1924 either reflected this movement or were essays on tyranny. Both variants were infused with the Expressionist characteristics of fate, destiny and doom.

Fritz Lang's contribution to this new intellectual *Aufbruch* included *Destiny* (1921), a film of Expressionist atmosphere, which with Lang's architectural sense overcame the flat linear qualities of *Caligari* by achieving a more three-dimensional effect. In October 1924 Fritz Lang visited the United States for several weeks to observe film production techniques in New York and Hollywood. When they arrived in New York, he and Erich Pommer were detained aboard ship for several hours. Lang remembers:

> 'Erich and I were considered enemy aliens and for some such reason we couldn't land in New York on the day that the boat docked there but had to wait until the following day to disembark. That evening I looked from the ship down one of the main streets of New York and saw for the first time the flashing neon signs lighting up the street as if it were daytime. This was all new to me. I said to myself, what will a big city like this, with its tall skyscrapers, be like in the future? That started me thinking about *Metropolis*.'

The overall message of *Metropolis*, which was released in 1927, has been a subject of some controversy. This is not really surprising when one considers that the script was co-written by Lang, whose left-wing views were positively anti-Nazi, and by his wife Thea von Harbou, whose right-wing views enabled her to stay on in Germany to become a successful screenwriter for the Third Reich. The end product tackles the political problem of Capital versus Labour; in this case a vast slave community dominated by a small élite, and the ensuing revolt. It then attempts to invent a solution to reconcile the opposing elements, by love conquering all, which even Lang admitted was monumentally naive.

Metropolis is a giant city of the 21st century. It is powered by enormous machines run by an army of almost robotized slave workers who live in subterranean hovels. The minority élite live above ground, in the 'eternal gardens' at the top of a maze of skyscrapers. There is one spark of humanity among the workers, a beautiful girl called Maria, who preaches love and understanding. Freder, the son of John Frederson, master of Metropolis, sees Maria at the garden gates surrounded by starving children and follows her into the workers' city. Frederson finds out and instructs his scientific adviser, Rotwang, to make a robot in Maria's image to gain the workers' confidence and to halt any possibility of a revolt. Rotwang creates the robot, but to further his own ends. His plot, however, works too well and the false Maria incites the workers into destroying the machines, and when the pumps cease the underground city is flooded. Maria and Freder manage to escape, save the workers'

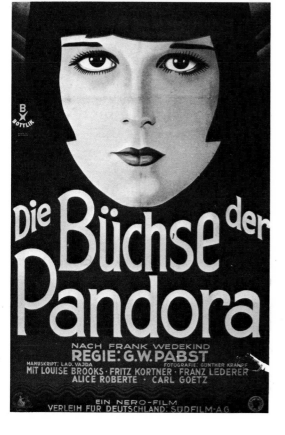

children, and the workers, realizing that they have been misled, burn the robot. Rotwang, seeing his plans ruined, goes mad. Frederson sees the errors of his ways and joins hands with Maria and Freder in front of the cathedral, uniting Capital and Labour through love.

The magnificent sets for *Metropolis* were designed by Otto Hunte, Erich Kettlehut and Karl Vollbracht, with sculpture by Walter Schultze-Mittendorf. The special effects were produced by Eugen Schufftan, inventor of the Schufftan process, an optical trick shot using mirrors to combine lifesize sets and miniatures. The elements of Expressionism that appear in Fritz Lang's film are echoed in the powerful

34 poster by Schulz-Neudamm, staff designer of the publicity department at Ufa. The head of Rotwang's robot is set against the mountainous architecture of the upper world and the dynamic title merges with the floodlit sky.

Brigitte Helm plays both Maria and the robot made in her image. The second

35 poster for *Metropolis* also echoes the futuristic side of the film, with Maria being prepared for transmutation.

The cameraman on *Metropolis* was Karl Freund, who in 1927 also collaborated with the documentary film-maker Walther Ruttmann on the making of what was to be

22 the first of the 'city symphonies' films, *Berlin-die Sinfonie Der Grosstadt*. Walther Ruttmann was born in Frankfurt in 1887. He studied painting, architecture and music and also became a successful designer of posters. Admiring the painter and avant-garde film-maker Viking Eggeling, he also became an early film experimenter and in 1924 created a nightmarish dream sequence about black hawks for Fritz Lang's films on the Nibelungen Saga.

Based on an idea by Carl Mayer, *Berlin-die Sinfonie Der Grosstadt* was inspired by Dziga Vertov's Kino-Eye principles (see page 44) and was a classic of rhythmic montage capturing the pulse and tempo of the German capital from dawn to midnight. The word 'symphony' in the title is significant. Ruttmann used the people in his film to form rhythms and patterns, the individuals themselves remaining anonymous. The dynamic opening uses symbolic imagery of pistons and wheels and then cuts to an early morning rail journey into the city, which is also intercut with shots of telephone lines, intertwining rails, stroboscopic bridges and landscapes of rural allotments and eventually the grey industrial city. The first views of the city show the deserted streets and empty factories, but as the city awakes, Ruttmann uses a whole series of montage effects, with opening shutters, windows and doors and machinery gradually gearing into action. The film continues with various sequences right through the working day, to the evening entertainments, the night-shift and the last buses and taxis.

In an interview for *Close-up* magazine, the photographer Karl Freund revealed that he had had the sensitivity of the film stock increased, in order to achieve candid camera and cinéverité results in any degree of lighting, and that he used various devices to conceal the camera from his subjects. This, he claimed, was photography in its purest form.

The poster for *Berlin-die Sinfonie Der Grosstadt*, which may have been designed by Ruttmann, also echoes the influences of Dziga Vertov, and is certainly similar to the Russian Constructivist posters of the Stenberg brothers, who in fact designed the Russian release poster for *Berlin* the following year. *Berlin* started a wave of 'city symphonies' to which Ruttmann himself later contributed with films on Dusseldorf, Stuttgart and Hamburg.

APPROACHING NEW REALISM

By the late 1920s German Expressionism had reached the compromise with Realism exemplified by G. W. Pabst's *Die Büchse de Pandora* (Pandora's Box) of 1929 which, even with Andre Andreyev's overwhelming, realistic sets, uses a visual landscape

Tartüff
Theo Matejko
1925

The hypocrite Tartüff is shown here lusting after Oregon in Matejko's graphic assimilation of the characters drawn from Molière's satire.

Metropolis
Schulz-Neudamm
1926
36½ x 83/92.7 x 210.9

The poster echoes the
elements of
Expressionism evident in
Fritz Lang's style and the
film's extraordinary sets,
designed by Otto Hunte,
Erich Kettlehut and Karl
Vollbracht.

Westfront 1918
Weber
1930

Prior to the National Socialists acceding to power in Germany a new mood, or 'New Objectivity', was emerging. In the graphic arts this found expression in the contemporary Art Deco style and is evident in this poster for Pabst's anti-war film.

based almost entirely on Expressionism. This compromise, encapsulating a growing feeling of cynicism towards society, was labelled *'Neue Sachlichkeit'* ('New Objectivity' or 'New Realism'). Pabst's *Pandora's Box* and *Diary of a Lost Girl*, made the same year, were also 'advanced' in their intimate concern with the sexual experiences of women. Both these films immortalized the American star Louise Brooks who, with her mixture of alluring sensuality and childlike innocence, gave the films their quality of decadent eroticism.

Pandora's Box was based on the plays *Erdgeist* (Earth Spirit) of 1893 and *Die Büchse der Pandora* of 1905, by Frank Wedekind. Louise Brooks plays Lulu, an extension of Pandora who, according to Greek mythology, was sent to Earth with a box containing all the world's ailments. Lulu is always surrounded by admirers, particularly the upright Dr Peter Schon, who is compelled by lust to marry her. He is accidentally killed when, after an affront to his honour, he tries to persuade Lulu to kill herself. Lulu is sentenced for his murder but escapes with Schon's now-infatuated son to London, where she crosses the path of Jack the Ripper.

The poster for *Pandora's Box* reflects Louise Brooks' allure, with her stylized *31* black helmet of hair presenting an image which is now more typical of Art Deco than Expressionism. It thereby reinforces the compromise of Expressionism with Realism and new movements in art.

Pabst's later films opposed the oncoming of National Socialism, including the anti-war films *Kameradschaft* (1931) and *Westfront 1918* (1930). The latter was Pabst's first talkie and, with its excellent feel for Realism and imaginative studio camerawork by Fritz Arno Wagner, is amongst the most frank and intolerant of anti-war films in the history of the cinema. The film is a study of men in the German trenches towards the end of the war and their coming to terms with life on leave, the routines between action and the horrors and mutilation at the front. Pabst's *'Neue Sachlichkeit'*, though predominantly studio bound, was in effect an anticipation of neo-Realism where, according to Siegfried Kracauer:

> 'Many shots betray the unconscious cruelty of the candid camera. Helmets and fragments of corpses form a weird still life; somewhere behind the front lines, several privates carry scores of wooden crosses destined to adorn soldier graves.'

Pabst himself felt that there was no need for romantic treatment. 'Real life is too romantic, too ghastly.' As an afterthought, Pabst added a giant question mark to the end title *of Westfront 1918*, which may well have infuriated the National Socialists, who in any event banned the film when they came to power. Like *Pandora's Box*, Weber's poster for *Westfront 1918*, with its highly stylized series of profiles of German *37* soldiers, has elements both of Expressionism and Art Deco.

The decline in German cinema began with the departure abroad of Ernst Lubitsch, F. W. Murnau, Paul Leni, E. A. Dupont and Erich Pommer. Although the transition to sound was no problem, owing to consistent experimentation in this direction, competition from Hollywood and the intrusion of American commercial interests affected production considerably. Nazi control began with their association with Alfred Hugenberg, Ufa's chairman of the board and a Hitler devotee. Expressionism and the *'Neue Sachlichkeit'* ceased to exist when the Nazis gained power in 1933.

WEBER F

WESTFRONT 1918
VIER VON DER INFANTERIE
EIN NERO-TONFILM
TOBIS

3 CONSTRUCTIVISM AND MONTAGE TOOLS OF THE RUSSIAN REVOLUTIONARY ARTISTS

The Art Nouveau and Expressionist movements had a negligible influence on the development of the Russian poster, which at the time employed a predominantly folkloristic style derived from the traditional peasant *lubok* woodcarving. It was not until 1908, when an avant-garde exhibition was held in St Petersburg, that the French and German Cubist and Abstract exhibits provoked a transition in the Russian aesthetic. The change was further stimulated by the Russian publication of Tommaso Marinetti's Futurist Manifesto, resounding '. . . the vibrant mighty fervour of arsenals and shipyards blazing with violent electric moons; greedy railway stations that devour smoke-plumed serpents . . .'. This homage to the machine and contempt for bourgeois values appealed to the revolutionaries among the Russians and Futurist forms began to appear. When Marinetti visited Moscow in 1914 the Russian Futurists, including Mikhail Larionov, Natalia Goncharova and Kazimir Malevich had issued their own Futurist and Rayonnist Manifestos.

The Cubists, particularly Juan Gris and Pablo Picasso, made considerable use of collage, from which the Russian artist Vladimir Tatlin (who had visited Picasso's studio in Paris) developed abstract hangings and relief constructions. Early in 1917 he was commissioned to design the interior of a basement theatre-café in Moscow, the Café Pittoresque, with the aid of Alexander Rodchenko, and this became a rallying point for Soviet artists. In 1920 he designed his 'Monument to the III International', an iron spiral framework about 1300 feet high, with counter-rotating central sections which were to house lectures, conferences and an information centre. This unrealized project was a pure example of Constructivism, echoing the ideas of the Futurists Archipenko and Boccioni that movement in space, not volume, was important in art.

These developments were not altogether politically neutral. As the politicians and theorists were working towards a new social order, so were artists and designers seeking a basis for producing a socially useful art of real materials in space, similar to

Man with the Movie Camera
Georgii and Vladimir Stenberg
26 x 41/66.4 x 104.5
1929

The Stenberg brothers utilized Constructivist principles in the production of dynamic compositions. In this case, the dramatic perspective and spiralling motion draw the eye into the poster.

the work of the engineer. These Constructivist concepts emerged through the Realist Manifesto produced by the brothers Naum Gabo and Antoine Pevsner and the Productivist Manifesto of Alexander Rodchenko and his wife Vavarna Stepanova, which were posted in the streets of Moscow in 1920. In the case of the film poster designer, his aesthetic was to be based on the actual techniques of film.

Lazlo Moholy-Nagy, in the Constructivist Manifesto of 1922, stated that:

> 'The new world of the masses needs Constructivism because it needs fundamentals that are without deceit.'

In 1924 the Leningrad Central Cultural Organization (Proletkult) recognized Constructivism as the authoritative style.

REVOLUTION AND THE FILM INDUSTRY

Conditions in Russia after the October Revolution were chaotic, causing many veteran film-makers to leave for other climates and restricting normal film production. Nonetheless, on November 9th 1917 the Bolsheviks set up a film subsection, *kinopodotdel*, as part of the newly-formed State Department of Education. This subsection was headed by Lenin's wife, Nadezdha Krupskaya. Its purpose was to reconstruct the film industry and turn it into an instrument for enlightening the working masses. Private film industrialists, who were enjoying a current boom in the cinema, boycotted the new state-owned theatres. Raw film stock became scarce and film production consequently suffered. Nevertheless, the embryonic ideology of the *kinopodotdel* developed its own full-grown socialist propaganda with the first agit-train leaving for the Eastern Front in 1918. These trains were specifically equipped to disseminate propaganda in the form of agitational entertainment, including films, plays and readings. Film crews travelled on the agit-trains to record events for *agitki* (propaganda films). Eduard Tissé (who later became Eisenstein's renowned cameraman) was aboard the first agit-train and the footage he shot was returned to Moscow and edited by the young film experimenter, Dziga Vertov. Many poster artists found work producing *rospisi*, or frescoes, on the wooden sides of the carriages; they included Dmitry Stakhevich Orlov (known by his signature as D. Moor) whose poster *Have you volunteered?* of 1920 was the most famous during the civil war.

Film stock mysteriously reappeared when the government nationalized the film industry in August 1919 (which took effect in January the following year). Lenin's belief that 'of all the arts, for us cinema is the most important' led to the formation of Proletkino in 1923 to produce political films in line with Party ideology. All private film companies were dissolved and a state monopoly of film production and distribution was declared. This organization, called Goskino (and after 1926 Sovkino), had its own poster department, Reklam film. Its appointed head was the artist designer Yakov Rukhlevsky, who soon assembled a group of poster designers, most of whom were former students from Vkhutemas (the Higher Art Studios in Moscow), including the Stenberg brothers, Nikolai Prusakov, Aleksandr Naumov, Mikhail Dlugach, Leonid Voronov, Grigory Rychkov, Grigory Borisov, Iosif Bograd and Iosif Gerasimovich. Most of the early films produced at Proletkino were conventional, and Party opinion varied on the validity of the avant-garde. However, in July 1925 the Politburo was resolved against hindering the affairs of artistic style.

CONSTRUCTIVISM AND PHOTO-MONTAGE

Photo-montage originated in the experiments of the early 19th century photographers and was revived during the First World War by Georg Grosz and John Heartfield in their Surrealist, and later politically oriented Dada, works in Berlin. Raoul Haussmann, founder of the German journal *Der Dada*, experimented with the arrangement of cut-out photographs, or photo-montage, in 1918.

> 'This process was called photo-montage because it embodied our refusal to

Battleship Potemkin
1905
Alexander Rodchenko
1925

Rodchenko's adaptation
of the dramatic images in
Eisenstein's classic film
produces a dynamic
composition firmly based
in the Constructivist
ideal.

Fragment of an Empire
Georgii and Vladimir
Stenberg
24½ x 37⅛/62.3 x 94.2
1929

The poster image
represents the man in
Friedrich Ermler's film
who, having lost his
memory during the Civil
War, regains it ten years
later and is duly
bewildered by the
extensive social changes
he perceives.

play the role of the artist. We regarded ourselves as engineers, and our work as that of construction: we assembled our work, like a fitter.'

Berlin Dada evolved from the original wartime movement in Zurich and from the Novembergruppe, whose painters had exhibited in Moscow by arrangement with El Lissitsky, Professor of Architecture and Graphic Art at the School of Fine Arts in Vitebsk. Russian artists who had visited Berlin found a common ground with Dada and by 1922 the movement was well-known. Photo-montage immediately became the tool of Constructivist artists and designers, who believed that this new form of plastic art was related to the development of industrial culture.

Lev Kuleshov, who was given a workshop at the State Film School, began to implement his own theories of montage. Pudovkin, who had worked in Kuleshov's workshop, explains:

'Kuleshov maintained that the material in film-work consists of pieces of film; and that the method of composing is their joining together in a particular creatively conceived order. He maintained that film-art does not begin when the artists act and the various scenes are shot – this is only the preparation of the material. Film art begins from the moment when the director begins to combine and join together the various pieces of film. By joining them in various combinations, in different orders, he obtains differing results.'

Sergei Eisenstein, who became the master of film-montage, published his initial ideas in the 1923 *Lef* (Left Front of the Arts) magazine in connection with his theatrical production *Enough Simplicity in Every Wise Man* at the Proletkult Arena (a new workers' theatre).

'The basic materials of the theatre arise from the spectator himself – and from our guiding the spectator into a desired direction (or desired mood), which is the main task of every functional theatre (agit, poster, health education, etc.). The weapons for this purpose are to be found in all the left-over apparatus of the theatre (the 'chatter' of Ostuzhev no more than the pink tights of the prima-donna, a roll on the kettledrums as much as Romeo's soliloquy, the cricket on the hearth no less than the cannon fired over the heads of the audience). For all, in their individual ways, bring us to a single ideal – from their individual laws to their common quality of attraction.

I establish attraction as normally being an independent and primary element in the construction of a theatrical production – a molecular (i.e. compound) unity of the efficiency of the theatre and of theatre in general. This is fully analogous with the 'pictorial storehouse' employed by Georg Grosz, or the elements of photographic illustration (photo-montage) employed by Rodchenko.'

EISENSTEIN AND RODCHENKO

Eisenstein joined the Red Army in 1918 and painted posters, *rospisi* and caricatures for the agit-trains. Released from the army in 1920, he went to Moscow and there joined the staff of the Proletkult Arena. After producing various plays, the collective decided to produce a series of films called *Towards the Dictatorship (of the Proletariat)*. The fifth film in the series, and the only one to be made, was Eisenstein's *Strike* (1925). The success of *Strike* and the realization of the potential in film convinced Eisenstein that he should continue to work in this medium. Remaining at Proletkult would mean dividing his attention between theatre and film. He therefore resigned and went to work at the Moscow studio of Serzapkino. His first assignment was to prepare a film on the First Cavalry Army's role in the civil war. However, for the twentieth anniversary of the 1905 Revolution, Eisenstein was taken off this current project and given a huge script by Nina Agadjanova-Shutko, entitled simply *1905*. Eisenstein was ready to start shooting the short *Potemkin* section of the film. The sequence was to cover a strike of dock-workers, the demonstration after the

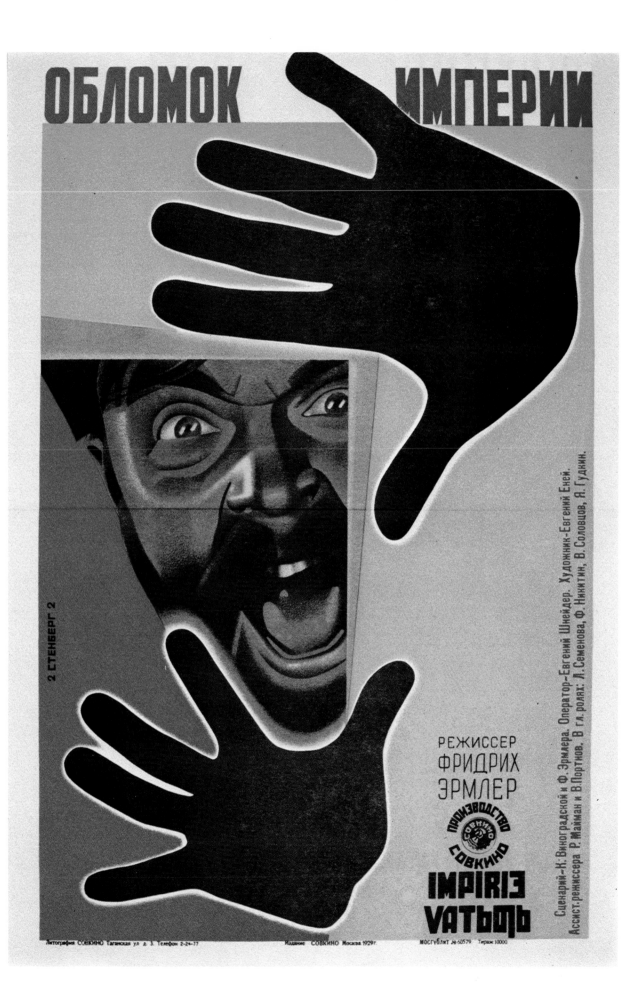

Potemkin mutiny and consequent events, in 42 shots. On seeing the vast flight of marble steps at Odessa's harbour, Eisenstein immediately visualized the scene for the Cossack massacre of the crowd.

> '. . . It was the very movement of the steps that gave birth to the idea of the scene, and with its 'flight' roused the fantasy of the director to a new 'spiralling'. And it would seem that the panicky rush of the crowd, 'flying' down the steps, is no more than materialization of those first feelings on seeing this staircase.'

It subsequently became apparent that this episode spoke for the whole Revolution and in the final cutting only the *Potemkin* section remained from the original *1905* script. From this evolved one of the most pure and concise examples of film structure.

Eisenstein used diagonal patterns to imbue his images with a dynamic force, reflected in Rodchenko's poster for *Battleship Potemkin*. Commissioned at Eisenstein's personal request, Rodchenko encloses the image of the battleship in a rhombus shape, which on continued viewing transforms into a titled square from which giant gun barrels thrust. The yellow title lettering is arranged vertically along the sides of the 'square' in contrast to the black outer lettering which is at right-angles to the 'rhombus'. This correlation between image and lettering gives the overall design an extraordinary visual dynamism.

41

Rodchenko, who was born in 1891, studied in Kazan and then in 1914 in Moscow, where he began his compass and ruler drawings. In 1915 he met Kazimir Malevich, who in 1913 had invented Suprematism, an ascetic form of Cubism and a totally pure geometrical abstract art. He worked with the writer Vladimir Mayakovsky, always at the hub of Soviet cultural activity, designing early revolutionary posters and participating in the Lef group from 1923 to 1925 and Novy Lef from 1927 to 1928. The *Lef* magazines were organs of the Constructivists, establishing innovations in montage and typography. Rodchenko's cover for the second issue of *Lef* was in montage, as was his book design in 1923 for Mayakovsky's love poem *About this*. Rodchenko also contributed to *SSSR na Stroyka* (USSR in Construction), of which Malevich was art director, and other illustrated periodicals and books. He was credited with designing the first dynamic film titles for Dziga Vertov's series of newsreels, *Kino-Pravda* ('Filmed truths'), integrating them into the films as elements in their construction, and produced Constructivist sets for Protazanov's science-fiction fantasy *Aelita* in 1924. Along with Tatlin and others he became a leader in industrial design, architecture, and by implication poster design, and helped shape the new order.

EYE AND THE CAMERA

In January 1929 Dziga Vertov released the film *Man with the Movie Camera*. Although the film uses a dawn-to-dusk framework, it differs from Ruttmann's *Berlin* and other city symphonies by commenting more on the relation between film and reality. The actual city scenes are cursory and filmed at random and we are constantly made aware of the cameraman. The film includes split screens, multiple superimpositions, variable speeds and a scene where people are watching the same film as we are, all used to support the director's Kino-Eye theory.

Vertov was associated with the aim of the Futurists, including Mayakovsky . . . . 'to expose to workers the bourgeois structure of the world.' During the civil war he was in charge of photographic work for the Partisan army led by Kozhevnikov, including the filming of *The Battle of Tsaritsin* and *Anniversary of the October Revolution*. Subsequently, at the age of 22, he was established as head of the Cinema Department of the All Russia Central Executive Committee with responsibility for the total Soviet newsreel output, *Kino-Pravda*. Vertov believed that the camera eye was more perfect than the human eye:

'I am eye. I am a mechanical eye. I, a machine, am showing you a world the likes of which only I can see. I free myself today and forever from human immobility . . . . I apparatus, manoeuvering in the chaos of movements, recording one movement after another in the most complex combinations . . . My road is towards the creation of a fresh perception of the world. Thus I decipher in a new way the world unknown to you.

The utilization of the camera, as a cinema eye – more perfect than the human eye for purposes of research into the chaos of   MAKE WAY FOR
visual phenomena filling the universe.   THE MACHINE

The eye lives and moves in time and space, perceiving and recording impressions in a way quite different from the   DOWN WITH
human eye. It is not necessary for it to have a   16 PHOTOGRAPHS
particular stance or to be limited in the number   PER SECOND
of moments to be observed per second. The
movie camera is better.

We cannot make our eyes better than they have been made, but the movie camera we can perfect forever.'

The image of the camera was also a compelling one for the poster designer and is used in two widely contrasting posters for *Man with the Movie Camera*, both
53   designed by the Stenberg brothers. The first is a montage of various elements: the juxtaposition of movie camera and machine guns fixed to tripods, both representing weapons; the half-face of the girl linked to the dancing legs through the camera and
38   tripod; and the camera eye as that of the girl's own left eye. In the second poster the dancing girl, still fragmented, is now superimposed onto a background of towering buildings, drawn in a worm's-eye perspective. The film's credits, which are formed into two circles, symbolize the lens of the camera. There is an overall ambiguity where the linking of the larger curved title to the outer circle gives an impression of spiralling motion and the dancing girl now looks like a figure falling from the top of a skyscraper.

THE STENBERG BROTHERS

Vladimir Stenberg was born in 1899 and his brother Georgii a year later. Sons of a Swedish-born artist, they studied at the Moscow School of Applied Arts and in the first independent state studios. With Medinetzky in January 1920, they published the manifesto *Constructivists of the World* to coincide with a Moscow exhibition. They began designing film posters in 1923. In 1925 they visited Paris and received the Gold Medal for theatre design at the Art Deco exhibition, where they met Larionov, the Futurist painter. In 1926 they organized the First Film Poster Exhibition at the Kamerny Theatre in Moscow. Together they designed approximately 300 film posters. According to Szymon Bojko in *New Graphic Design*, they enlarged portions of cinema frames and still photographs through a projector for the basis of their work.

46   The Stenbergs' poster for Friedrich Ermler's *Katka's Reinette Apples* of 1926 surrounds the girl's face with flights of stairs on which two men are conspiring. The film concerns a young girl, Katka, who goes to Petrograd in the first days of the NEP (New Economic Policy) to find work. She is, however, reduced to selling apples in the street, where she encounters the city's underworld. Seduced, cheated and abandoned, she finally meets the gentle Fyodor. The designers use the idiom of the cinema, unusual camera angles, close-ups and montage, to produce the symbolic imagery of the trapped heroine.

THE MANUFACTURED IMAGE

On March 16th 1929 Grigori Kozintsev's and Leonid Trauberg's *The New Babylon*

A Kiss From Mary Pickford
Semion Semionov
1927

Semionov's amusing poster is for a film starring the Soviet comedian Igor Ilyinsky and edited footage featuring Mary Pickford and Douglas Fairbanks taken at random whilst they were visiting Moscow.

Katka's Reinette Apples
Georgii and Vladimir Stenberg
1926

A flight of stairs, blocked by two men, top and bottom, was chosen by the poster designers to symbolize Katka's predicament.

Bureaucrats and People
Nikolai Prusakov
1929

Prusakov often juxtaposed elements of photo-montage and caricature in forms reminiscent of the Dadaists.

The Living Corpse
Grigory Borisov and Pyotr Zhukov
1929

Aware of the power that letter forms had given to the French Cubist and Italian Futurist works, the Russian poster designers utilized typography as a basic design element to great effect, particularly evident in this striking poster.

was released. Elena Kuzmina plays Louise Poirier, a sales-girl in a luxurious Parisian department store, the 'New Babylon'. Through her eyes we see contrasting sectors of French society; the poor with whom she lives and the rich people she serves and for whom she works. The climax of the film portrays their contrasting attitudes towards the German advance on Paris, when the rich bargain and capitulate and the poor become patriots sacrificing themselves for their capital. Defending the city, they find themselves in a position of authority and establish a city government. This heroic tragedy of the Paris Commune was photographed by Moskvin and his assistant Mikhailov and has been described as one of the most sardonic of Soviet films. Characters from contrasting strata of French society flash across the face of Louise
48 Poirier in Iosif Gerasimovich's poster, drawing the viewer into the dynamic atmosphere of the film.

Vsevolod Pudovkin appears in a tiny role as a salesman in *The New Babylon*, but stars as Fedya Protasov in the German-Soviet co-production of 1929, *The Living Corpse*. This, the third cinema version of Tolstoy's play, was directed by Fyodor Otsep. Shooting began in Moscow for exterior locations and gypsy scenes and was completed in Berlin with the non-Russian cast, Maria Jacobini and Gustav Diessl. Although Pudovkin seems to have left directorial control to Otsep he probably had a hand in the editing. Pudovkin also directed such classics as *Mother* (1926) and *Storm Over Asia* (1928).

47 The poster for *The Living Corpse* was designed by Grigori Borisov and Pyotr Zhukov. Use of typography as the basis of design had now reached its peak. The title credits are repeated as an overall pattern, forming a screen through which the ethereal figure of the 'living corpse' is pointing. Borisov was a member of the Young Artists Society and specialized in film posters, working frequently with Zhukov, Naumov and Prusakov.

Nikolai Prusakov designed the poster for Leonid Leonidov's and Yakov Protazanov's *Bureaucrats and People*, also of 1929. The film is a collection (an innovation not repeated for over ten years) of three Chekhov short stories. Prusakov was another exponent of photo-montage with a particular interest in automobiles, which appear in his posters for *Five Minutes that Shook the World* and *Great Tragedy of a Small Woman*. His poster for *Bureaucrats and People* is a montage featuring a
46 portrait of a woman wearing an inverted cabriolet as a hat. It also includes a four-faced mask (for each of the Chekhovian characters as performed in the film by Moscow Art Theatre actor Ivan Moskvin); and a pince-nez. Prusakov exhibited at Obmokhu (Young Constructivist Artists) in 1919 and 1921 and the First Film Poster Exhibition of 1926. In 1928 he organized the Second Film Poster Exhibition. He lectured on art at the Moscow Institute of Applied Art and designed jointly with Borisov and Naumov.

Viktor Turin's *The Turksib Railway* (1929) describes the actual construction of the Turkestan-Siberian railway in narrative terms, producing a dramatic masterpiece of
51 documentary. Semion Semionov's poster employs montage in the construction of a cartoon-like figure from elements of railway signals, human hands, face and feet. Semionov also designed the one humorous poster illustrated here, for the 1927 film *A Kiss from Mary Pickford*. Douglas Fairbanks and Mary Pickford were on a visit to Moscow, which culminated in Fairbanks taking Eisenstein's *Potemkin* to the United States, with invitations for Eisenstein to follow. Whilst in Moscow they were randomly filmed by the Kuleshov graduate Sergei Komarov and the edited footage was used to
46 make the film, which starred the celebrated Soviet comedian Igor Ilyinsky. The poster is divided into three planes, splitting the two major portraits in half, into colour and monochrome. The wheels of Fairbanks' inverted bicycle link the two 'colour' eyes of both portraits.

Other poster designers included Anton Lavinsky, who was head of the sculpture department at Vkhutemas and created the political ROSTA posters (the abbreviation

The New Babylon
Iosif Gerasimovich
1929

The heroic tragedy of the Paris Commune is represented in this dynamic poster by the films' characters flashing across the face of the leading protagonist, Louise Poirier, sales-girl of the luxurious Parisian department store, The New Babylon.

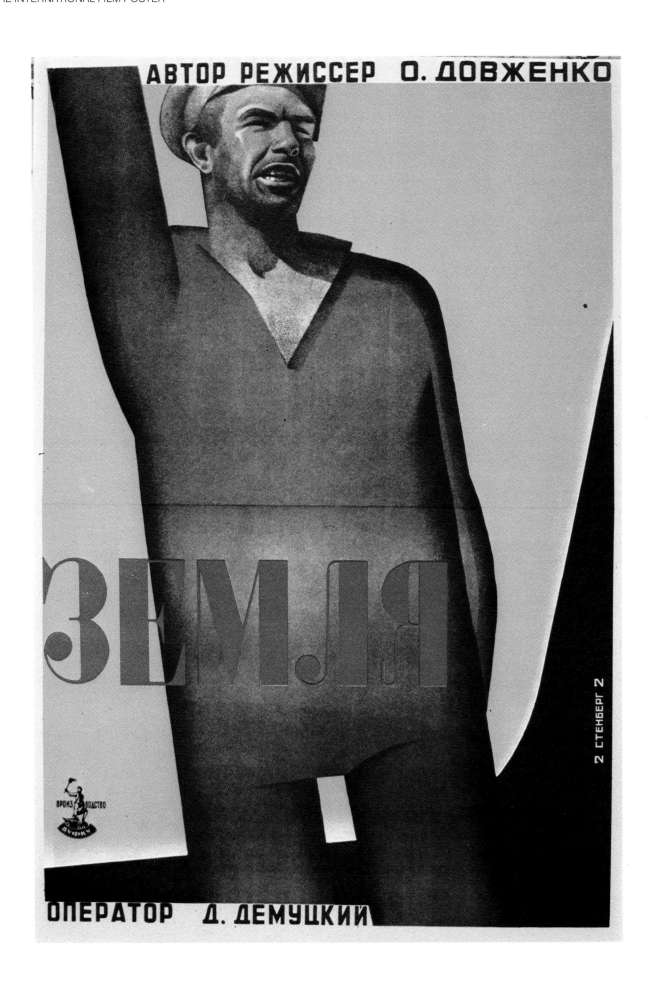

Earth
Georgii and Vladimir
Stenberg
1930

The Stenberg brothers
were masters of
composition, sometimes
using one powerful
image, which in this case
conveys the simplicity of
Dovzhenko's
masterpiece.

Turksib
Semion Semionov
1929

The construction of the
Turkestan-Siberian
railway is here
represented in montage
form to produce a
cartoon-like figure from
railway signals, a human
face and limbs.

The Conveyor of Death
Nikolai Smoliak
1934

Although Stalin's
doctrine of Socialist
Realism stifled the
cinema and poster
design, a few
Constructivist designs
still appeared.

**Man with the Movie
Camera**
Georgii and Vladimir
Stenberg
1929

The Stenbergs use
elements of symbolism
in this second design for
Vertov's film, drawing a
parallel between the
movie camera and the
machine gun as tools of
the revolution.

for the Satire Window of the Russian Telegraph Agency) and an alternative poster for
Eisenstein's *Potemkin*. Leonid Voronov (nicknamed 'the fireman' because of his
speed of execution) and Mikhail Ievstayev produced a striking poster for Eisenstein's
October in 1928. It was designed in two panels, with a zigzag white line linking them
through the italic title, incorporating a livid green portrait of Trotsky and illustrations of
Menshevik anarchist women and members of the provisional government in a car.
The illustrations were taken directly from stills of the film.

By 1928, debates had begun about the failures and accomplishments of the
films produced for the new social order. Eisenstein's *October* was received with
hostile suspicion by Party leaders. An All-Union Party conference on cinema, held on
March 15th 1928, resolved that 'the basic criterion for evaluating the art qualities of a
film is the requirement that it be presented in a form which can be understood by the
millions'. This had a repressive effect on posters as well as films. Although the
Stenbergs' poster for *Earth* is a striking design, compared to their earlier work there is
a hint of a more traditional style of representation. Stalin's stranglehold on the Party,
which soon embraced the cinema, stifled the spirit of creativity before sound films
became established. He had withdrawn the licence to create revolutionary art and the
era of Socialist Realism, which would dominate Soviet cinema till after his death, had
begun.

50

4 THE HOLLYWOOD DREAM MACHINE
THE ZENITH OF COMMERCIALISM

The pioneers of the American film industry – the Edison Manufacturing Company, the American Mutoscope and Biograph Company and American Vitagraph Incorporated – were all based on the East coast. For twelve years they dominated the industry, which was bedevilled by lawsuits initiated by Thomas Edison over what he considered to be patent infringements. In 1908, the year that marked D. W. Griffith's first film at Biograph, these and seven other companies founded the Motion Picture Patents Company to bring to an end the long-standing court battles. The newly-formed company then attempted to monopolize the film industry by various legally questionable methods which, in the end, brought about its own demise through the provisions of the Sherman Anti-trust Act. By 1918 the company no longer existed.

In 1907, Colonel William Selig had transferred part of his Chicago-based Selig Polyscope Film Company to Los Angeles and two years later established the first large West Coast film studio. Others were to follow. Close to Los Angeles, and surrounded by orange groves, was the peaceful small town called Hollywood. It was while out searching for suitable film locations that Cecil B. De Mille, co-partner of the Jesse L. Lasky Feature Play Company, came to the end of the railway line and there discovered this idyllic town. He acquired a large stable, converted it into a studio and commenced production. De Mille was followed by a migration of independent producers all determined to escape the stranglehold of the Patents Company. By 1920 Hollywood had become the focus of the film industry, producing around 800 films a year, its name synonymous with glamour, affluence and dreams of stardom.

EARLY COMPETITORS

In 1910 the Patents Company had organized a distribution branch, the General Film Company, to distribute each member's films to licensed theatres. Immediately, General Film contracted with the A. B. See Lithograph Company of Cleveland to

Gold and Glitter
41 x 81/104 x 206
1912

This early full-colour stone lithograph was printed by the A. B. See Lithograph Company of Cleveland for General Film, a subsidiary of the Motion Picture Patents Company, of which Biograph was a member. D. W. Griffith produced hundreds of films for Biograph (including *Gold and Glitter*) before leaving for Reliance-Majestic in 1913 and the potential freedom of production chief. Two years later the Biograph company was dissolved as part of the court action taken against the Motion Picture Patents Company on anti-trust legislation.

Woman
Burton Rice
1918

A highly graphic poster by Burton Rice for a film by Maurice Tourneur, one of the leading stylists of American silent cinema.

produce posters for each film. To maintain individual company identity, ABC (as they were known in the trade) printed posters with stock borders in two or three colours incorporating the company's trade-mark. Onto the central area of these posters were printed the title of the film, a plot synopsis and a photograph supplied by the producer. The photos were usually taken by the film cameraman during production. The General Film Company would then sell the posters to the nickelodeons at 15 cents each.

Independent lithographers fought against this monopolization by printing their own full-colour stock posters, using various dramatic scenes common to many movies of the time. Many exhibitors preferred these, even when the poster image had nothing to do with the actual film. This practice continued through to the 1930s, when some very fine stone lithographs were printed. The Harold Lloyd poster for *Professor Beware* (1938) bears the following clause: *63*

> 'Notice: This advertisement was not produced by the maker or distributor of the motion picture bearing the title appearing thereon and no one represents that this scene actually appears in the said motion picture.'

Competition from these 'pirate' companies forced ABC to improve the quality of their own posters, evident in the 1912 sheet for *Gold and Glitter*, a one-reel film directed by *54* D. W. Griffith for Biograph.

Biograph also spawned the talent of Mack Sennett, who was directed by Griffith in many short films between 1908 and 1911. By 1910 he was already directing his own shorts and starring in them himself. Sennett's success enabled him to form his own production company with the backing of two former bookmakers, Charles O. Bauman and Adam Kessel, resulting in the formation of Keystone. His growing number of stock performers included Roscoe 'Fatty' Arbuckle, Chester Conklin, Mack Swain, for a time Charlie Chaplin, and of course the Keystone Kops, represented by the amusing British poster on page 59. *59*

Griffith's last film for Biograph was *Judith of Bethulia* (1913), America's first four-reel film, and his own response to Enrico Guazzoni's Italian Biblical epic of 1912, *Quo Vadis?*, which had been booked into the Astor Theatre in New York by George Kleine, with the admission price set at one dollar, a new high at that time. Kleine, co-founder of the Kalem production company, had been the prime mover in influencing Edison to form the Patents Company and save profits being wasted in lawsuits.

The one company member to survive the effects of the anti-trust court decisions was Vitagraph, which had already established a studio in East Hollywood in 1913 and continued to prosper until its eventual sale to Warner Brothers in 1925. The exquisite poster illustrated on page 58 is for an unknown film and has been specifically *58* produced for the European market, hence the title in three languages. Vitagraph's early stars included Norma Talmadge, Adolphe Menjou and Rudolph Valentino.

THE STARS APPEAR

With the dissolution of the Patents Company (and General Film with it) producers sought better posters for their new five-reel features. These posters were distributed through their own exchanges or through agencies which rented them out for a modest fee. Some sheets were backed with muslin and could be reused indefinitely. The Patents Company producers had refrained from adding their stars' names to posters for fear of being asked for higher salaries. Consequently, Florence Lawrence, who worked for Biograph, was called simply 'The Biograph Girl'. In 1910, the independent rebel producer Carl Laemmle, who had defied the Patents Company by setting up his own production company, lured Lawrence away from Biograph and anonymously spread the rumour that 'The Biograph Girl' had been killed in a streetcar accident in St Louis. The next day he placed a notice in the newspapers condemning these vicious reports and announced that Miss Lawrence was now working for him.

Le Génie du Mal/Der Geist des Bösen/Il Genio del Male
39 x 55/98.7 x 139

Vitagraph, founded in New York in 1896 by two British immigrants, J. Stuart Blackton and Albert E. Smith, survived the aftermath of the court action against the Patents Company, of which it was a member, and flourished until its take-over by Warner Brothers in 1925. Its early lead in film production and its continued success at home and abroad necessitated the printing of posters with a blank space for tri-lingual titles. Vitagraph posters were easily identified by their splendid trademark.

We Have Always on Hand a Keystone Comedy
28½ x 38½/72 x 98
c. 1912–1915

A stock British poster advertising the company famous for its madcap Keystone Kops and the first films featuring Charlie Chaplin.

To prove that she was indeed alive, Laemmle sent her to St Louis, where she was duly mobbed by the crowds. This ingenious publicity stunt promptly launched the star system. Posters now began to feature the stars' faces with scenes from their films, and their names were printed in type much larger than that used by the originally pre-eminent production companies. D. W. Griffith was one of the few directors of this period whose name was used on posters in preference to those of his stars. Even for *Way Down East*, made in 1920, Griffith's name was reckoned to be more of a draw *62* than the film's star, Lillian Gish. The dramatic poster on page 62 depicts Richard Barthelmess rescuing her in the climactic and hazardous ice-floe sequence.

Now that the star system was well under way, the studio bosses became impatient with the time taken to create new stars and began to import existing ones. The distribution in America of Sarah Bernhardt's *Queen Elizabeth* in 1912 was a great success for Adolph Zukor. Three years later the Lasky Feature Play Company brought the opera star Geraldine Farrar to Hollywood and in 1917 starred her in *Joan the* *66* *Woman*, which became an early classic for Cecil B. De Mille (another director whose name always appeared prominently on posters). Lasky's Company merged with Zukor's Famous Players at this time, but before its eventual growth into Paramount, the new company, Famous Players-Lasky Corporation, produced many films with notable stars, such as Mary Miles Minter, who made *The Heart Specialist* in 1923. *63*

More mergers were on the way and in 1924 the Metro Picture Corporation, the Goldwyn Picture Corporation and Louis B. Mayer Pictures merged to form Metro-Goldwyn-Mayer. In its first year of production King Vidor, later to make the highly acclaimed films *The Big Parade* and *The Crowd*, directed *The Wine of Youth* with Ben *61* Lyon and Eleanor Boardman, who plays a girl courted by two suitors but afraid of marriage through the quarrelling of her parents.

Most of the major studios were now distributing their own advertising material (known as 'paper' in the trade). When the exhibitor collected his film print he would also receive a great variety of posters: 11″ x 14″ lobby cards in sets of eight; 22″ x 28″ half-sheets; 14″ x 36″ insert cards; 27″ x 41″ one-sheets; 41″ x 81″ three-sheets; 81″ x 81″ six-sheets and billboard-size posters. Quite often the exhibitor had no space to display all these and may well have been showing the film for only one day anyway. Additionally, 14″ x 22″ window cards could be obtained for hanging in shop windows and other small high street businesses, and would be displayed in exchange for free passes to the cinema. For a standard film of the 1910s, three-sheets, six-sheets and billboard posters were plastered everywhere. One-sheets were seldom used for theatre front display; by contrast, this is standard procedure today.

COLOUR PRINTING

The technique of offset printing was used in the production of posters before the turn of the century, utilizing a system of printed dots to produce tone: the bigger the dot, the darker the tone. It could not, however, produce the fabulous range of colours required by the studios; the only other way to achieve these was by stone lithography. The 'stones' were initially made from Bavarian limestone, but after the First World War zinc and aluminium plates became the norm. Skilled craftsmen separated the artwork supplied by the studio into its individual colour components. Solid tones, including letters, were painted directly onto the stone by the engraver with a waxy ink. A greasy crayon was then used to draw on the half-tones, their strength controlled by the density of the crayon. Acid mixed with gum arabic was afterwards applied to the stone and then rinsed off, to leave the parts treated with ink and crayon standing out in relief. This formed the printing plate onto which the printing ink would be rolled. Only the areas covered in wax would pick up the ink, which would then be printed onto the paper. Each colour needed a separate stone, so a poster like *The Ghost of Slumber* *67* *Mountain*, printed by the Butts Litho Company of New York, may well have used eight

Salomé
22 x 28/55.9 x 71.1
1922

A luminary of the
Broadway stage, Alla
Nazimova began in 1921
to produce progressive
adaptations of famous
plays for the screen,
including Dumas'
Camille and Ibsen's *A
Doll's House.* In her
audacious adaptation of
Oscar Wilde's *Salomé*,
represented by this
Beardsleyesque poster,
she went completely
over the top. The film was
generally disliked and
she soon returned to the
stage.

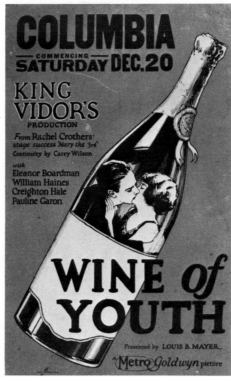

Wine of Youth
14 x 22/35.6 x 55.9
1924

The poster for King
Vidor's first MGM
production uses a simple
visual metaphor to
illustrate the film.

Way Down East
27 x 41/68.6 x 104.1
1920

After *Birth of a Nation* and *Intolerance*, D. W. Griffith became a household name. He always featured prominently on his posters, in place of the films' stars.

Quo Vadis?
14 x 22/35.6 x 55.9
1912

An early example of a window card, used for hanging in shops and small high street businesses. This imported Italian biblical epic induced D. W. Griffith to reply with his own *Judith of Bethulia* in 1913.

The Heart Specialist
27 x 41/68.6 x 104.1
1923

One of the last films made by the popular star Mary Miles Minter, who briefly rivalled Mary Pickford. Her career was wrecked by her involvement, along with Mabel Normand, in the unsolved homicide of the director William Desmond Taylor. The subsequent revelations of his sex life destroyed Minter's demure screen image.

Professor Beware
27 x 41/68.6 x 104.1
1938

Pirate printing companies often vied with the major operators by producing extremely colourful alternatives to the commissioned posters which often were not up to standard. The practice continued into the 1930s, even after the major studios had acquired their own distinctive styles.

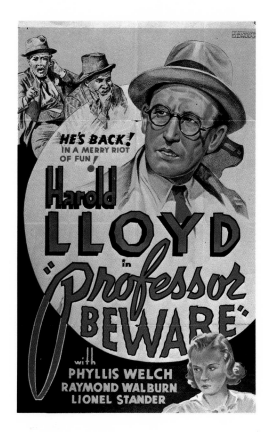

separate plates. Even though the larger three-sheet, six-sheet and especially twenty-four-sheet posters were designed to be seen from a distance, and could therefore afford to be somewhat coarser, using fewer plates, the quality remained extremely high.

The Ghost of Slumber Mountain was a two-reeler made by Willis O'Brien, creator of *King Kong*, in 1918. The film was an early experiment in model animation concerning a mountain climber who falls asleep and dreams that he meets the bearded ghost of an old hermit who once lived on the mountain. The ghost reveals a magic telescope which shows life on the mountain as it was millions of years ago. Distributed by the World Film Corporation, the film was a tremendous success, grossing over $100,000 from an initial investment of $3,000.

DEVELOPING TECHNIQUES

During the 1910s, lobby cards, insert cards, window cards and half-sheets were mainly printed in brown-and-white rotogravure. Some colouring may have been done by hand or by stencil, but the images were basically pale reproductions of photographs. The examples shown on pages 70–71 are: Carol Dempster in D. W. Griffith's *Dream Street* (1921); Mary Pickford in *Little Lord Fauntleroy* (1921); and *Little Annie Rooney* (1925); Ben Turpin in *The Shriek of Araby* (1923); Harold Lloyd in *For Heaven's Sake* (1926) and Enrico Guazzoni's *Quo Vadis?*. 70-71 63

In the 1920s, some posters had progressed to using cut-out effects, setting the image of the star in deep colours and fine detail against a white, or imaginary background. The poster for Douglas Fairbanks' *The Black Pirate* (1926) uses a cut-out of Fairbanks and his adversary against a white background with a non-realistic seafaring scene at their feet. The poster also includes two photos, formed into flag shapes, and a laughing caricature of Fairbanks. *Steamboat Bill, Jr.* (1928) shows Buster Keaton and Ernest Torrence cut-out against a white background, with a circular photographic scene, bordered by a drawn life-belt, centred between them. Cut-outs were also used to great effect in lobby cards — a feature which has continued in one form or another to the present day. In the 1925 films *Don Q, Son of Zorro* and *The Eagle*, both Douglas Fairbanks and Valentino feature full-length in black and white against a white background in the border. The action is taken up by the main photograph. 69 69 71 70

The process of photogelatin, or heliotype, introduced in the 1920s, has been used in all subsequent printing of lobby cards. A metal plate covered with photosensitized gelatin is exposed to light through a normal photographic negative. The gelatin then hardens in relation to the amount of light it receives; the denser the image, the harder it becomes. The darkest areas absorb more ink and produce the darkest tones when printing. Although the process was occasionally used for printing one-sheets, it was specifically used for the smaller posters and lobby cards which were to be viewed from close up. It was originally a monochrome process, moving to two and then three colours. The standard colours of bright pink, yellow and a purplish-blue were duller than those used in lithography.

Printing and paper were relatively cheap and the studios ordered posters with abandon. Most of the big releases had two designs for one-sheets: style 'A' and style 'B'. The 'A' style would usually be a portrait of the star, whilst the 'B' style would show the star and co-star together. Posters like *The Kid* (1921) and *Son of The Sheik* (1926), shown on page 76, would probably be only one of many designs proposed for these major releases. Professional artists were used more and more, but they were not allowed to sign their work or produce a style that would be recognizable as their own. The rare exceptions include Burton Rice's Art Nouveau design for Maurice Tourneur's *Woman* (1918) and the poster for Alla Nazimova's 1922 modernist version of *Salomé*, designed in the style of Aubrey Beardsley with a simplicity reflected in the 76 57 61

Art Deco sets of the film and the costumes designed by Natasha Rambova. Posters for comedy films gave the artists opportunity for caricature, as can be seen in the illustration on page 75 for the Marx Brothers' *Duck Soup* (1933).

75

Throughout the 1930s, 40s and 50s, the smaller posters from all the studios were very similar, little reflecting the individual styles created for their one-sheets. The MGM one-sheet for *Song of the Thin Man* (1947) has a mainly white and pale yellow background with the faces of William Powell and Myrna Loy (and Asta the dog) while a speech balloon contains the credits and slogan. The insert card for *Shadow of the Thin Man* (1941) is crowded with faces of Powell and Loy, who are also seen full-length walking Asta, with various scenes at top and bottom. The credits and title fill the rest of the poster. The RKO one-sheet for *Citizen Kane* (1941), apart from one red and one blue stripe, has a white background with the artwork in pale washes. The half-sheet poster for the same film uses the same artwork in heavier colours against a bright yellow background, together with fairly large photos of scenes from the film.

77

77

77

The serial became internationally popular with *The Perils of Pauline*, starring Pearl White, in 1914. In 1920 Edward Sedgwick, brother of another serial queen, Eileen Sedgwick, directed *Bride 13*. The poster for Chapter 14 illustrates a 'pit and the pendulum' scene (see page 75). Serials dropped in production with the advent of sound but did not diminish in popularity. The studios which dominated the field of sound serials were Universal, Republic, Columbia and Mascot. In 1931 Mascot produced a 12-Chapter serial featuring Boris Karloff called *King of the Wild*. The poster illustrated on page 75 is for Chapter 5 'The Pit of Peril'. Both posters are extremely vivid stone lithographs, *Bride 13* being printed by the Otis Litho Company of Cleveland, a mid-western town renowned for printing theatrical paper.

75

75

Individual printing companies left their stamp on memorable posters, and on poster development in general. In 1918, Rupert Julian directed, and took the title role in, *The Kaiser – The Beast of Berlin*. The poster is quite unusual for its period, showing a highly stylized portrait of the Kaiser in black helmet, with a green, orange and blue face and rectangular yellow eyes pouring forth laser-like light, against a fiery red background. The title is in raised lettering of bright blue. In 1925, Julian directed Lon Chaney in *The Phantom of the Opera*. The subject matter once again lends itself to a certain amount of stylization, with the huge red, green and blue image of the Phantom towering over the Paris Opera. Both these posters were printed by the Morgan Litho Company of Cleveland, one of the major stone lithographic printers. Another example, shown on page 74, is for Clarence Brown's *Smouldering Fires* (1925). Morgan introduced colour offset lithography as the silent era gave way to sound (a major event in cinema history which had little or no effect on poster design). This process meant that the artwork could be photographed through screens that would separate the colours mechanically. Although the rich tones of stone lithography could not be produced this way, the overall effect was much clearer and this obviously faster process replaced stone lithography over the next two decades.

76

76

74

BILLING

The single star poster faded as more studios co-starred their players, introducing the new problem of billing, where one name must always precede the other. If two stars shared equal status then one might have his or her name billed second on the poster, but would feature more prominently in the artwork. Unequal status led to agents demanding specific sizes of lettering on the posters, so cramping artistic style.

In 1927, John Gilbert starred in *Flesh and the Devil*, with Greta Garbo and Lars Hanson as featured players. Even though each role was of equal importance, their names were printed in much smaller type than Gilbert's. Garbo's rise to stardom necessitated equal billing with Gilbert the following year when they made *A Woman of Affairs*.

78

78

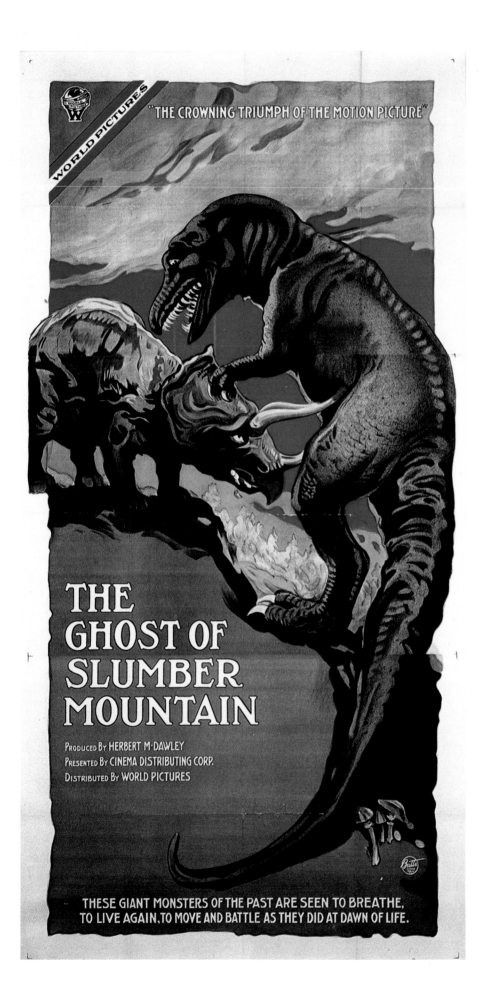

Joan the Woman
14 x 22/35.6 x 55.9
1917

Cecil B. De Mille's name always appeared prominently on posters, in this case with the diva Geraldine Farrar.

The Ghost of Slumber Mountain
41 x 81/104 x 206
1918

An important staging post for Willis O'Brien on the way to *The Lost World* (1925), his first feature-length fantasy employing stop-motion animation for its special effects. The poster is a fine example of stone lithography at its best. Posters larger than one-sheet size could afford to be printed somewhat coarser as they were to be viewed from a distance. However, the printing on this three-sheet is extremely vivid. Known posters for *The Ghost of Slumber Mountain* also include one-sheets and six-sheets, making a lot of paper for a film that lasted approximately 16 minutes. Nevertheless, the investment paid off handsomely.

CONTRASTING STYLES

With the advent of three-strip Technicolor in 1933, the studios insisted that poster artists now used colours true to those in the film. More and more colour films were being made but the design studios still only received black and white photographs to work from; the idea proved unworkable and was quickly abandoned.

By the late 1930s, the larger studios had developed their own style of one-sheet design (this also applied to three-sheets, six-sheets and billboards). The poster artwork for RKO (a company which can be traced back to 1909 and through the First World War as the Mutual Film Corporation) was rendered in warm watercolour washes with splendid portraiture, typified by *La Cucaracha* (1934). In the 1940s, Val *79* Lewton produced a series of low-budget horror films for RKO that have become minor classics. The posters for these films all have dense backgrounds with bold, bright title lettering, always at an angle or in a curve. Deep greens and blues dominated and the image would invariably present a female being menaced by someone or something. Two such posters from 1943 are *The Leopard Man* and *I* *78* *Walked with a Zombie*.

MGM's posters were, in contrast, bright and simple. Quite often a semi-portrait of the star (or stars) would be used against a monochrome background without detail. *Anna Christie* (1930) and *Libeled Lady* (1936) are prime examples. MGM was the first *82,8* studio to use offset lithography extensively in the 1930s, although stone lithography was still occasionally employed till the later 40s. Most MGM work was done by the Tooker Litho Company. The examples illustrated of posters for musicals are mainly from MGM, who specialized in this genre. Their one-sheets for *It Happened in* *80* *Brooklyn* (1947) and *Singin' in the Rain* (1952) both have white backgrounds with simple designs of the stars' faces or the stars dancing, and the one-colour title in a slight arc. The Paramount one-sheets for *Blue Skies* (1946) and *Lady in the Dark* *83,8(* (1944) not only illustrate the stars, but include dancing scenes and various other details from the films. There is virtually no white as the backgrounds are full coloured. However, the smaller MGM posters for *Barkleys of Broadway* (1949) and *Band* *81* *Wagon* (1953) are even busier than the Paramount posters. The Morgan Litho Company, pioneers of offset lithography, converted Paramount to this process in the 1930s, producing such posters as *Zaza* (1939) with Claudette Colbert, which is *82* similar to the earlier MGM posters but features bolder colours.

Fox, who used Tooker Litho, persisted with stone lithography right up to the early 1950s, despite the higher costs. Their posters look extremely busy, including every colour imaginable, portraits of stars and featured players and scenes from the film. A typical example is the poster for *Mysterious Mr Moto* (1938) with Peter Lorre. *82*

Posters for Warner Brothers are certainly the odd ones out, being printed mainly in two colours and using photographs instead of original art. Although the crudest in design of all the studios, they are very effective for the kind of film we now associate with Warners: the Bogart/Cagney gangsters and thrillers such as *The Roaring 20s* *87* (1939), *Taxi!* (1932), *Casablanca* (1943) and *Passage to Marseille* (1944); the Errol *85,8,* Flynn vehicles including *They Died With Their Boots On* (1942) and detective films *84,8!* such as *The Kennel Murder Case* (1934) with William Powell. For some reason many of the images on the Warner posters were taken from different films. For instance, the Bogart image in *The Maltese Falcon* (1941) is not that of Sam Spade, private *85* investigator, but gangster Roy Earle from the earlier *High Sierra* of the same year. Slogans had been used on posters right from the start, but in such usually unimaginative and meaningless forms as 'The Season's Laugh Treat' or 'It's so Romantic'. Warners' posters, however, have been consistently inventive in using a few words to tell the public exactly what to expect, as in *The Great Lie* (1941) with Bette Davis and George Brent: 'There are some things a woman has to lie about . . . to a man!'; and Errol Flynn's character in *Rocky Mountain* (1950): 'Part renegade, part

Steamboat Bill Jr.
22 x 28/56 x 71
1928

The Black Pirate
22 x 28/56 x 71
1926

RUDOLPH VALENTINO in "THE EAGLE"

The Eagle
11 x 14/28 x 36
1925

Don Q, Son of Zorro
11 x 14/28 x 36
1925

A popular treatment in
small posters of the
1920s was the cut-out
device.

The Shriek of Araby
11 x 14/28 x 36
1923

Little Lord Fauntleroy
11 x 14/28 x 36
1921

Dream Street
11 x 14/28 x 36
1921

Little Annie Rooney
11 x 14/28 x 36
1925

For Heaven's Sake
11 x 14/28 x 36
1926

Various examples of
lobby cards from the
1920s printed in brown-
and-white rotogravure.
All these cards, apart
from *Little Lord
Fauntleroy*, have been
colour tinted either by
hand or by stencil.

hero . . . a rebel whose guns turned treason into glory . . . for his captive Yankee girl!'

The poster campaigns were organized through the advertising offices in New York. Stills were sent over from Hollywood, or the art directors would read the scripts and simply imagine some of the scenes. In the silent days, one artist would design the entire poster, but in the 1930s different artists were used for layout, lettering and illustration. One-sheet posters were usually painted to the same size, but the bigger posters were mechanically enlarged. The poster companies themselves employed artists to produce material for the smaller studios such as Republic and Monogram. One example is the poster for *Paradise Canyon* (1935), an early John Wayne vehicle for Monogram.

Anonymity was still the rule, but well-known artists would occasionally be hired to design a specific poster and these were sometimes signed. Vargas, the famous pin-up artist, gave Betty Grable a great deal of publicity in his poster for *Moon Over Miami*   *91* in 1941. Thomas Hart Benton designed a poster for *The Grapes of Wrath* (1940) and Norman Rockwell, famed for his paintings in the *Saturday Evening Post*, designed posters for, amongst others, *The Magnificent Ambersons* (1942) and *The Song of Bernadette* (1943).

THE STAR IMAGE

If the star of the film was a Harlow, Dietrich, Lake, Hayworth or Monroe, it mattered less to portray what the story was about when it came to designing the poster. Jean Harlow was playing bit parts when she was given the chance to play the English girl in Howard Hughes' First World War aerial spectacular, *Hell's Angels* (1930). She replaced the heavily-accented Swedish star Greta Nissen, who was playing the part before Hughes decided to re-shoot the film for sound. Harlow's seduction of Ben Lyon and her platinum blonde hair caused a sensation, although the poster depicts her as having dark blonde tresses. The poster for *Public Enemy* (1931) shows her with   *91* red hair, and in fact the only poster available that highlights the platinum blonde image is for the film *The Girl from Missouri*, which was made in 1934. When she switched to   *90* MGM, Harlow found a talent for light comedy; her acting ability was finally acknowledged and she quickly became a superstar. The poster for *Libeled Lady*, made in 1936, shows the glamorous image toned down.

Marlene Dietrich just was *The Scarlet Empress* (1934) and Paramount saw no reason to put anything else on the poster but her. Even before *The Blue Angel* (1930) was released in Germany, Paramount brought Dietrich to Hollywood in 1930 to co-star with Gary Cooper in Josef von Sternberg's *Morocco*. (1930) The poster says it all: Dietrich embracing her legionnaire lover Cooper against a desert background. Following his own success in *The Winning of Barbara Worth* (1926), Gary Cooper was featured in the film *It* (1927), which was a showcase for the 'It' girl Clara Bow.

The poster for Preston Sturges' satirical comedy *Sullivan's Travels* (1942) shows   *89* Veronica Lake (who later the same year caused quite a stir when she teamed up with Alan Ladd for *This Gun for Hire*) as a provocative blonde in red evening gown, even   *88* though for most of her screen time she is disguised as a hobo. Rita Hayworth co-starred as a platinum blonde in Orson Welles' intricate thriller *The Lady From*   *89* *Shanghai* (1948). There is nothing intricate about the poster, however, which reflects the studio's doubts about Welles and the public's adoration of Rita Hayworth. Unfortunately, Marilyn Monroe's rise to stardom came at a time when the quality of poster art was deteriorating. Even though the poster for *Niagara* (1953) is quite   *92* effective, and that for *The Seven Year Itch* (1955) uses the legendary shot of her skirt   *93* blowing up, the artwork for most of her other films is undistinguished.

ON THE BANDWAGON

Science fiction became very popular in the 1950s and although Universal had three

96
96

96

decades of experience in the genre, producing classics such as *The Incredible Shrinking Man* (1957), the other companies were all determined to cash in. William Cameron Menzies made *Invaders from Mars* for Fox in 1953 and just about everything in the film is crammed into the poster. On the other hand, the poster for the MGM film *Forbidden Planet* (1956) suggests something more than the film had to offer.

The studios were also trying to exploit the medium in the face of heavy competition from television and sought to re-awaken interest in various 3-D processes as a possible solution to dwindling cinema audiences. Most of the actual films were poor, however, and the whole experiment fizzled out within a few years. The posters did their best to sell the gimmick, as can be seen in the illustration for *The*
96   *Maze* (1953).

Saul Bass

The late 1940s saw a liberalization in the attitude to blacks in films. One of the first to depict a black hero pitted against a bigoted white was Joseph Mankiewicz's *No Way*
103   *Out* (1950), where Sidney Poitier, in his first Hollywood film, plays a hospital intern who becomes the focus of controversy when a patient, the brother of an hysterical racist played by Richard Widmark, dies. This film also marked the emergence of a highly distinctive style in film poster design, and the man responsible was Saul Bass. Bass was born in New York in 1920, studied at the Art Students' League and Brooklyn College and became a freelance designer, eventually forming Saul Bass and Associates, Inc. in Los Angeles in 1946. The evident appeal of his graphic work to Otto Preminger brought him a job as film title designer for Preminger's *Carmen Jones* in 1954. His evocative animated titles revolutionized film credits and Preminger
98,101 continued to use him for such films as *Man with the Golden Arm* (1955), *Saint Joan*
99 (1957), *Bonjour Tristesse* (1957), *Anatomy of a Murder* (1959), *Exodus* (1960), *Advise*
102 *and Consent* (1963) and *The Cardinal* (1962), for which he also produced film posters. Extracting a basic symbol from his credit titles, Bass interpreted the nature of the film in simple graphic terms, making his posters instantly recognizable and striking. Bass
100 also worked on the title credits for Hitchcock's *North by Northwest* (1959), *Psycho* (1960) and *Vertigo* (1958), and from the last derived a spiral symbol which he embodied in this now-classic poster. He produced equally distinctive posters for films
102 on which he did not work as title designer, including *Death of a Salesman* (1951), *Love in the Afternoon* (1956) and the humorous *One, Two, Three* (1961) for Billy Wilder.

Smouldering Fires
14 x 22/35.6 x 55.9
1924

All window cards were
printed with a wide top
border so that the theatre
name and show dates
could be overprinted
when convenient. This
fine stone lithograph
depicts a party
sequence, where the
much older wife (played
by Pauline Frederick)
becomes agonizingly
aware of the youth of her
husband and his friends.

King of the Wild
27 x 41/68.6 x 104.1
1931

Bride 13
27 x 41/68.6 x 104.1
1920

Another area where films
were represented by
relatively large quantities
of posters was the serial.
Not only did companies
produce the variety of
sizes for each film, but
each chapter had its own
range of posters. A
standard serial such as
The Perils of Pauline was
in 20 chapters, but *The
Hazards of Helen*,
produced during 1914 to
1917, reached a
staggering 119
episodes.

Duck Soup
22 x 28/55.9 x 71.1
1933

The anarchic comedy of
the Marx Brothers
enabled artists to
produce some classic
caricature imagery for
their film posters, in
particular this stylized
design.

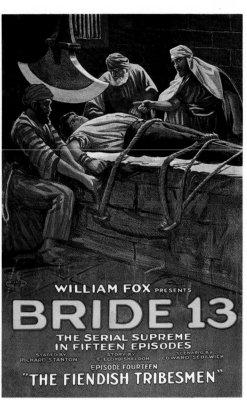

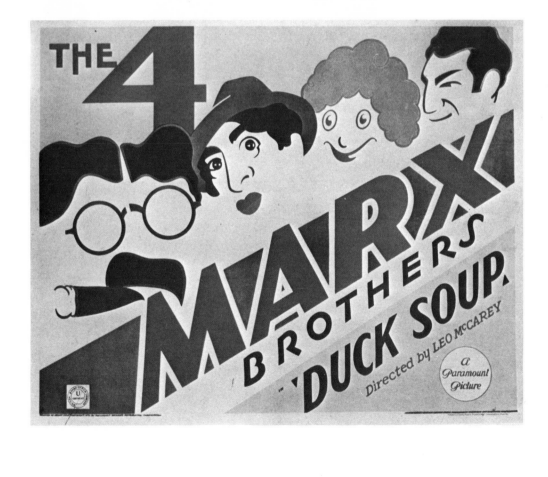

The Kid
27 x 41/68.6 x 104.1
1921

This highly acclaimed first feature-length film by Chaplin was also successful at the box office, ranking second only to Griffith's *The Birth of a Nation*. The large financial investment and long production schedule (it took 18 months to film and cost $500,000) would certainly have led to a publicity campaign producing many different one-sheet designs.

The Son of the Sheik
27 x 40/68.6 x 101.6
1926

After separating from his second wife, Natacha Rambova, who had been the dominant influence in his career from 1921, Rudolph Valentino went on to make two highly successful films, *The Eagle* and *The Son of the Sheik*, before his sudden death from a perforated ulcer in 1926.

The Kaiser — the Beast of Berlin
14 x 22/35.6 x 55.9
1918

The Phantom of the Opera
81 x 81/206 x 206
1925

Two Lon Chaney films, both directed by Rupert Julian. In *The Kaiser — the Beast of Berlin* Chaney played Admiral von Tirpitz (the versatile Julian was in the title role). *The Phantom of the Opera*, made at the height of Chaney's fame was the peak of his career as an actor and genius of make-up.

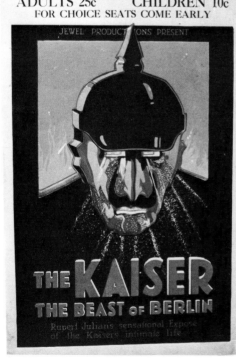

Song of the Thin Man
27 x 41/68.6 x 104.1
1947

Shadow of the Thin Man
14 x 36/35.6 x 91.4
1941

Citizen Kane
27 x 41/68.6 x 104.1
1941

Citizen Kane
22 x 28/55.9 x 71.1
1941

During the 1930s, 40s and 50s when the major studios were developing their individual one-sheet styles, their smaller posters remained quite similar.

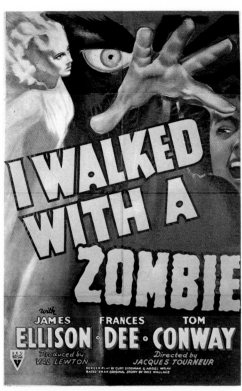

Flesh and the Devil
27 x 41/68.6 x 104.1
1927

A Woman of Affairs
22 x 28/55.9 x 71.1
1928

Garbo, tired of playing 'vamps', was nevertheless persuaded by MGM to portray another in *Flesh and the Devil*. This one concession to the studio bosses fortunately combined her talents with those of Clarence Brown, who became her favourite director. The film made her a top star and although she was billed second to the current romantic idol John Gilbert, in her next film, *A Woman of Affairs*, also directed by Brown, they shared equal billing.

I Walked With a Zombie
27 x 41/68.6 x 104.1
1943

The Leopard Man
27 x 41/68.6 x 104.1
1943

In contrast to the warm shades of *La Cucaracha*, the dense colouring and vivid lettering of *The Leopard Man* and *I Walked With a Zombie* evoke the moody atmosphere of the short string of B horror masterpieces produced at RKO between 1943 and 1946 by Val Lewton.

La Cucaracha
27 x 41/68.6 x 104.1
1934

The first live-action, three-colour Technicolor production.

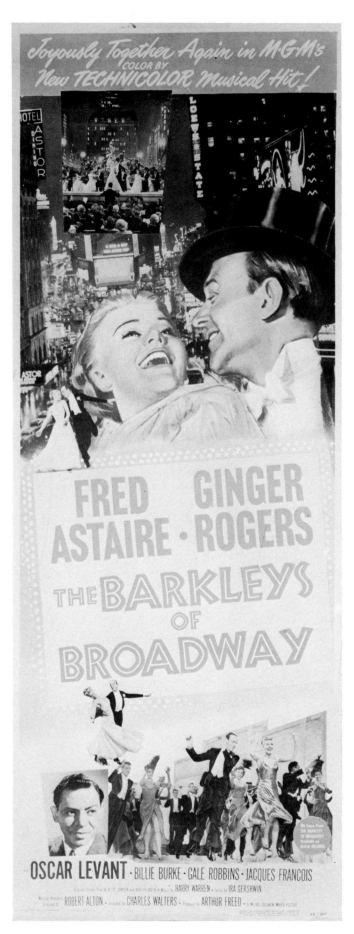

Singin' in the Rain
27 x 41/68.6 x 104.1
1952

It Happened in Brooklyn
27 x 41/68.6 x 104.1
1947

Although they account for only a portion of MGM's total output, the studio is mainly associated with its musicals of the late 1940s and early 50s. Under the guiding hand of producer Arthur Freed, with such stars as Fred Astaire, Gene Kelly, Judy Garland and Frank Sinatra, and directors Vincente Minnelli and Stanley Donen, the studio could do no wrong. MGM's one-sheet posters caught the vitality of the period with a spirited gaiety, using bright colours and simple designs against a white background.

Barkleys of Broadway
14 x 36/35.6 x 91.4
1949

Band Wagon
22 x 28/55.9 x 71.1
1953

These smaller posters from MGM, unlike the one-sheets, are crammed full of images.

Libeled Lady
27 x 41/68.6 x 104.1
1936

Libeled Lady, a scintillating comedy, featured four of MGM's leading stars, Jean Harlow, Spencer Tracy, William Powell and Myrna Loy, all illustrated here in a typical MGM one-sheet.

Mysterious Mr Moto
27 x 41/68.6 x 104.1
1938

Fox's continued use of stone lithography led to some extremely colourful posters in which white backgrounds were almost non-existent.

Anna Christie
27 x 41/68.6 x 104.1
1930

Garbo's first talkie, once again directed by Clarence Brown, was a tremendous hit.

Zaza
27 x 41/68.6 x 104.1
1939

Paramount's pre-war one-sheets were similar to those of MGM but used bolder colours.

Blue Skies
27 x 41/68 x 104.1
1946

Paramount's *Blue Skies* featured over two dozen Irving Berlin songs (four of them specially written for the film) and reunited Bing Crosby and Fred Astaire for the first time since *Holiday Inn* (1942). The one-sheet for this film and for *Lady in the Dark* (page 86) are extremely busy, portraying the stars and all sorts of scenes from the films against coloured backgrounds.

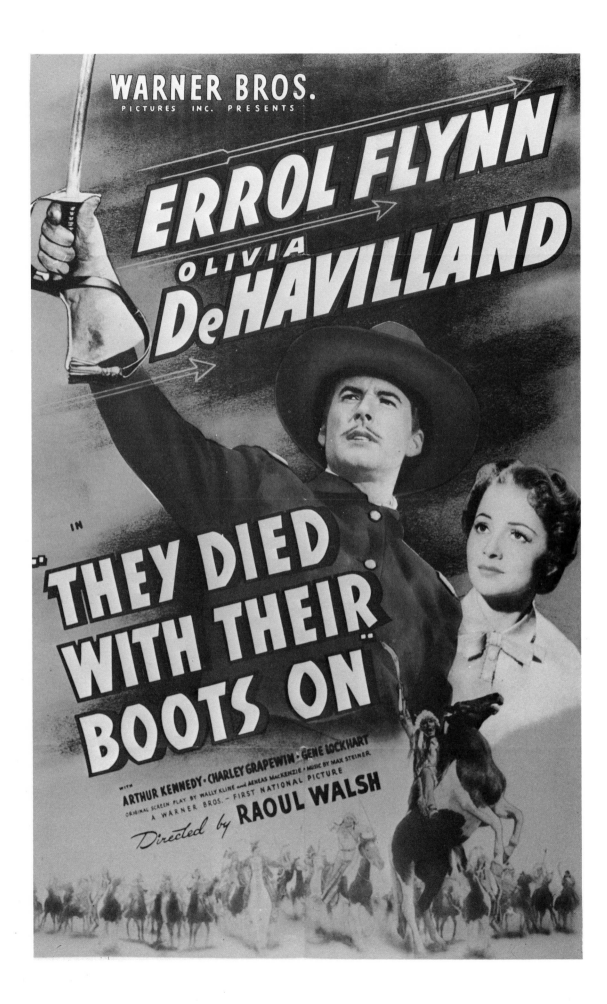

They Died With Their Boots On
27 x 41/68.6 x 104.1
1942

The Kennel Murder Case
27 x 41/68.6 x 104.1
1934

Taxi!
14 x 22/35.6 x 55.9
1932

The Maltese Falcon
27 x 41/68.6 x 104.1
1941

Passage to Marseille
27 x 41/68.6 x 104.1
1944

Warner Brothers' posters differed considerably from those of the other studios, employing photographs and one or two colours in their one-sheets to dramatic effect, but reversing the norm by applying more artwork to the smaller posters and less photography.

Lady in the Dark
27 x 41/68.6 x 104.1
1944

Lady in the Dark was a
sumptuous-looking but
watered-down version
of the Moss Hart-Kurt
Weill 'psychological'
musical in which Ginger
Rogers reveals her
fantasies on psychiatrist
Barry Sullivan's couch.

The Roaring Twenties
22 x 28/55.9 x 71.1
1939

Casablanca
22 x 28/55.9 x 71.1
1943

This Gun For Hire
27 x 41/68.6 x 104.1
1942

Sullivan's Travels
27 x 41/68.6 x 104.1
1942

Whatever role the leading stars enacted in their films, the studios unhesitatingly depicted them to best advantage in their publicity. Veronica Lake is disguised as a tramp throughout most of *Sullivan's Travels* yet she appears on the poster as the same sultry blonde portrayed in *This Gun For Hire*.

The Lady From Shanghai
27 x 41/68.6 x 104.1
1948

Part thriller, part confusing commentary on Welles' marriage to Rita Hayworth, *The Lady from Shanghai* ran way over budget and further angered Columbia by portraying the lovely Rita as a heartless monster. The poster for the film determinedly stresses Hayworth's more glamorous attributes.

Moon Over Miami
Alberto Vargas
14 x 36/35.6 x 91.4
1941

With a few notable exceptions, American film poster artists have almost always remained anonymous. Among the exceptions was the famous pin-up artist Alberto Vargas, whose skills were put to use in various posters including *Behave Yourself* with Shelley Winters, *The Flame of New Orleans* with Marlene Dietrich, *Suddenly It's Spring* with Paulette Goddard and, probably his best known, *Moon Over Miami*, spotlighting Betty Grable as the forces' number one pin-up girl of World War Two.

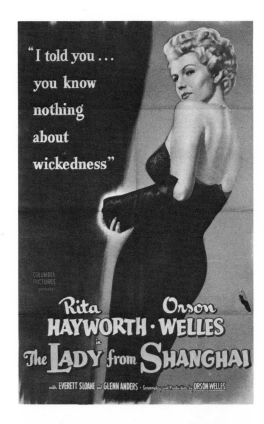

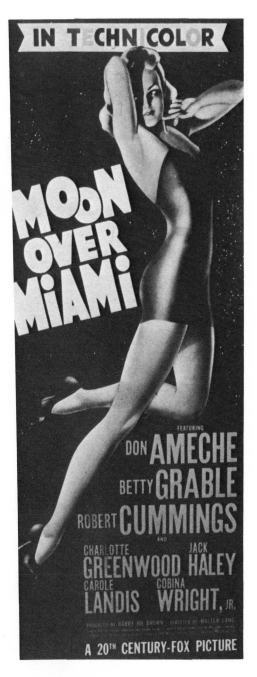

The Girl From Missouri
14 x 22/35.6 x 55.9
1934

Hell's Angels
27 x 41/68.6 x 104.1
1930

Although remembered
as the girl with the
platinum blonde hair,
Jean Harlow often
appeared dark blonde or
even red-haired. *The Girl
From Missouri*, in which
she played a
characteristic gold-
digging millionaire
hunter, gave the poster
artists an opportunity to
highlight the platinum
blonde tresses.

The Seven Year Itch
22 x 28/55.9 x 71.1
1955

Niagara
14 x 22/35.6 x 55.9
1953

Monroe's rising to
stardom when
Hollywood poster art
was on the wane meant
that very few posters
succeeded in doing
justice to one of the
screen's most
celebrated sex
goddesses. The two
examples illustrated here
are probably the most
successful.

Public Enemy
14 x 22/35.6 x 55.9
1931

Morocco
24 x 120/61 x 304.8
1930

The Scarlet Empress
14 x 36/35.6 x 91.4
1934

The image of Marlene
Dietrich as the
mysterious sado-
masochistic femme
fatale at the centre of
Josef von Sternberg's
extravagant tableaux
coincided exactly with
the heyday of Hollywood
poster design.

ROCCO

R, MARLENE DIETRICH
PHE MENJOU

ramount Picture

CTED BY JOSEF VON STERNBERG
APTED BY JULES FURTHMAN
E PLAY "AMY JOLLY" BY BENNO VIGNY

PALACE
THEATRE
ENTIRE WEEK, STARTING
SUNDAY, MARCH 27

CLARA BOW

An ELINOR GLYN —
CLARENCE BADGER
Production

"IT"

WITH
ANTONIO
MORENO

It
14 x 22/35.6 x 55.9
1927

The age of the flapper
was symbolized by Clara
Bow as the liberated
young woman who,
moulded by Hollywood's
publicity machine,
became known as the 'It'
girl.

The popularity of science fiction in the 1950s resulted in some memorable poster images.

Invaders From Mars
27 x 41/68.6 x 104.1
1953

The Incredible Shrinking Man
27 x 41/68.6 x 104.1
1957

Forbidden Planet
27 x 41/68.6 x 104.1
1956

The Maze
27 x 41/68.6 x 104.1
1953

William Cameron Menzies had a long and distinguished career as an art director (Fairbanks' *The Thief of Bagdad; Gone With the Wind; For Whom the Bell Tolls*) and a rather more erratic track record as a director, although the magnificent sets in Korda's *Things to Come* (1936) display his genius as a production designer. Nevertheless, *Invaders from Mars*, an intriguing low-budget science fiction feature (and later something of a cult film) and *The Maze*, an atmospheric exercise in Gothic horror, are lit with intermittent flashes of imagination and ingenuity.

Paradise Canyon
27 x 41/68.6 x 104.1
1935

Unlike the major Hollywood film studios, with their vast publicity and art departments, smaller companies relied on artists at the printing houses to produce designs for their films, with some exceptional results. This fine stone lithograph was produced for one of a long series of B Westerns made by John Wayne at Monogram in the 1930s.

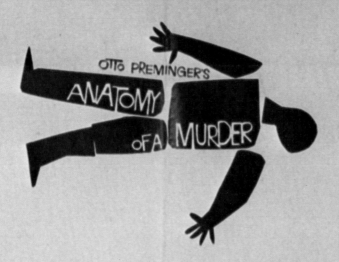

Saul Bass belongs to the generation of American designers, including Paul Rand and Bradbury Thompson, which emerged after the Second World War. He was a pioneer in the visual unification of motion picture graphics, capturing the film's theme in an elementary symbolic image and applying it to the film's advertising, credit titles and posters.

The Man With the Golden Arm
Saul Bass
30 x 40/76.2 x 101.6
1955

Anatomy of a Murder
Saul Bass
27 x 41/68.6 x 104.1
1959

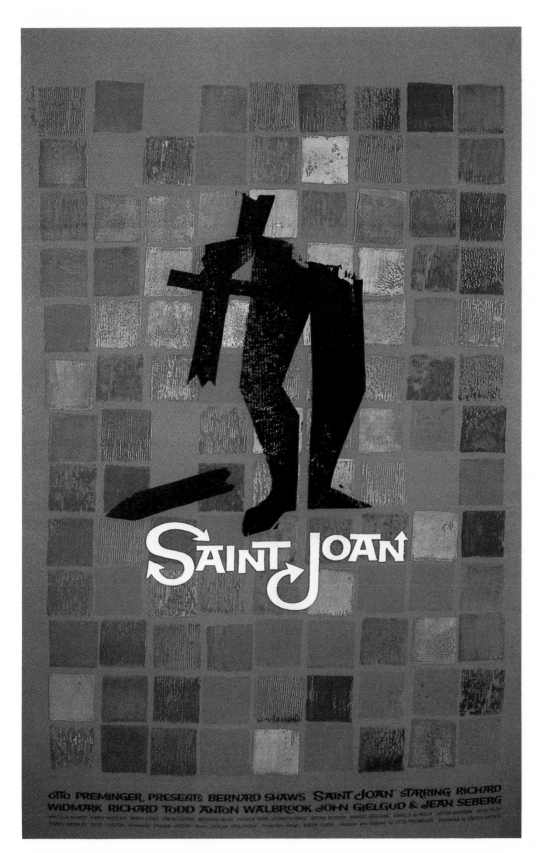

Vertigo
Saul Bass
27 x 41/68.6 x 104.1
1958

Saint Joan
Saul Bass
27 x 41/68.9 x 104.1
1957

Exodus
Saul Bass
30 x 40/76.2 x 101.6
1960

No Way Out
Saul Bass
22 x 28/55.9 x 71.1
1950

One, Two, Three
Saul Bass
30 x 40/76.2 x 101.6
1961

5 POSTERS GALORE! EALING STUDIOS AND THE PURSUIT OF EXCELLENCE

British cinema was born into the music hall and consequently utilized the same letterpress-style posters familiar to its patrons till around 1910, when pictorial posters came into general use. No particular style of design was achieved and from the late 1920s to the late 1930s, pictorialism vied with letterpress until the American style was revived.

It was in the late 1930s that Michael Balcon joined Basil Dean's Associated Talking Pictures at Ealing as head of production. Ealing Studios had been built by Dean in 1931 for ATP, but with its decline he returned to the theatre. One of ATP's directors, Reginald Baker, an old colleague of Balcon's, invited him to take Dean's place. With ATP's demise its subsidiary, Ealing Studios Ltd, became a production company.

In 1938, the year of his appointment, Balcon himself made Monja Danischewsky head of publicity. Their first years at Ealing saw five George Formby and five Will Hay comedies, six war films and other dramas and comedies, all exceptional films in themselves but not as yet fully stamped with the Ealing characteristics which are now so familiar. In 1943 Balcon produced *San Demetrio, London*, an heroic war film about a crew who abandon their burning tanker, spend three days adrift in a lifeboat, only to encounter the tanker again, miraculously still afloat, and so sail it back into the Clyde. *San Demetrio* marks S John Woods' appointment to Ealing's advertising department to effect the new enlightened policy launched by Danischewsky and already evident in such earlier posters as George Chapman's *The Ghost of St Michael's* (1941).

S John Woods was born in 1915 and trained as a graphic designer and painter, working for Fox in the 1930s and producing posters for the Old Vic, Covent Garden and Sadlers Wells. He also produced abstract painting and articles promoting abstract art and exhibitions. Danischewsky's idea of employing professional outside artists to create posters was immediately implemented by Woods, who engaged

Richard III
27 x 40/68.6 x 101.6
1955

London Film Productions occasionally followed the Ealing policy with posters designed by Tony Wysard, Arpad Elfer, Charles Mozley, Francis Marshall, and especially *Things to Come* by Kupfer Sachs. This unsigned poster for Olivier's highly successful film is also above par.

Polly
40 x 85/101.6 x 216
1921

**The Fight in the
Thieves' Kitchen**
40 x 85/101.6 x 216
1921

Both of these short films
are represented by
posters which prove that
Britain could produce
lithographs to the same
high standard as did the
Americans. *Fight in the
Thieve's Kitchen* was
one of a series of 12 half-
hour crime films narrated
by an ex-Chief Inspector
of police. *Polly* was one
of a series of 28 macabre
short stories.

Hue and Cry
Edward Bawden
30 x 40/76.2 x 101.6
1947

Directed by Charles
Crichton, *Hue and Cry*
was a charming fantasy,
set against the realistic
background of London's
bombsite wastelands,
which anticipated the
mood of the later classic
comedy *Passport to
Pimlico* (1949). This was
Bawden's first
commission for Ealing
Studios and was
produced with black and
white still photographs
as his only reference.

Painted Boats
John Piper
21½ x 27¾/54.6 x 70.5
1945

The artist John Piper
came under the influence
of abstract art in the mid-
1930s and began basing
his work on geometrical
shapes. With his wife,
Myfanwy Evans, he
founded *Axis*, a quarterly
review of abstract art, in
1935. The Second World
War brought about a
mood of introspection
amongst many painters
and Piper himself forsook
abstraction for romantic
and richly detailed
architectural studies, a
style from which this
poster is developed.

Morris Kestleman to design the poster for *San Demetrio, London*. In 1944 H. A. Rothholz was commissioned to design the poster for J. B. Priestley's fantasy *They Came to a City*, with surreal results, and in the same year Woods himself produced the Edwardian-style poster for *Champagne Charlie*, with drawings by Eric Fraser and the title lettering by Barnett Freedman. The design evokes the atmosphere of Edwardian music hall and reflects the popular song sheet covers of the time. This characteristic post-war nostalgia was also highlighted by Ealing's *Pink String and Sealing Wax* (1945), *Nicholas Nickleby* (1947), *The Loves of Joanna Godden* (1947) and *Kind Hearts and Coronets* (1949). This yearning for the past, particularly by men who had spent much of the war years abroad, was reflected in elements of folk art utilized in these posters, such as the fairground-style lettering exploited in *Champagne Charlie, Painted Boats* (1945), *Hue and Cry* (1947), *Pink String and Sealing Wax* and *The Ladykillers* (1955). 117

Painted Boats was a drama documentary about life on the narrow boats of England's canals. Its nostalgic but fresh approach is represented by John Piper's exquisitely designed poster. The intricate tracery surrounding the title comes from a rubbing of a slate tomb made by the artist. 109

S John Woods employed artists who, he believed, could evoke the particular mood of each film. Piper was already known socially to both Woods and Balcon and had previously designed *The Bells Go Down* poster for a film starring Tommy Trinder and James Mason about the auxiliary fire service, produced at the same time as Humphrey Jennings' classic *Fires Were Started* (1943). One of the first Ealing posters to combine drawings and photographs was Piper's *Pink String and Sealing Wax*, which includes a drawing of a Victorian street in Brighton and a photograph of Googie Withers as the murderess Pearl Bond.

Dead of Night, made the same year as *Painted Boats* and *Pink String and Sealing Wax*, was the second Ealing fantasy film (*The Ghost of St Michael's* was, of course, a wartime Will Hay comedy where the 'ghost' turns out to be an enemy agent). *The Halfway House* (1944) was the first 'real' ghost film and its poster, by Matvyn Wright, depicts the two ghosts of the film, Mervyn and Glynis Johns, in light brown with the human visitors and the Halfway House in blue. *Dead of Night* has become a classic of its kind and Leslie Hurry's nightmarish poster is a rare collectors' item, with its composition of supernatural scenes from the film, skeletons and coffins all overwhelmed by a gigantic bat and all in blues, greens and yellows. Robert Helpmann (who at the time was choreographer and principal dancer at Sadlers Wells) saw one of Hurry's exhibitions and brought him to the ballet, where he designed some macabre sets for *Hamlet* in 1942 and soon became well known. 113

In complete contrast to Hurry's haunted style, Edward Bawden in 1947 created an extremely cheerful poster for *Hue and Cry*, the forerunner of the classic Ealing comedies. The film features Alastair Sim, whose comic-strip stories are used by London crooks as a code which is accidentally deciphered by the irrepressible Harry Fowler. Comedy was a relief from post-war austerity and at Ealing came to full fruition with three films released in 1949: *Passport to Pimlico, Whisky Galore* and *Kind Hearts and Coronets*. The poster for *Passport to Pimlico* was designed by S John Woods, incorporating a cartoon by Nicolas Bentley and photos of four of the leading protagonists. Tom Eckersley's poster for *Whisky Galore* also combines drawings and photographs, with Joan Greenwood and Basil Radford (opponents in a fight to hinder officialdom from confiscating hundreds of cases of salvaged whisky) immersed in a giant whisky bottle dominating the tight little island of Todday. 109

119

James Fitton designed the poster for the classic Ealing comedy *Kind Hearts and Coronets*, where Dennis Price plays the disinherited member of a titled family resolved to eliminate all the other members who stand between him and the dukedom. The colourful poster represents his final choice between the titled Edith d'Ascoyne and his 115

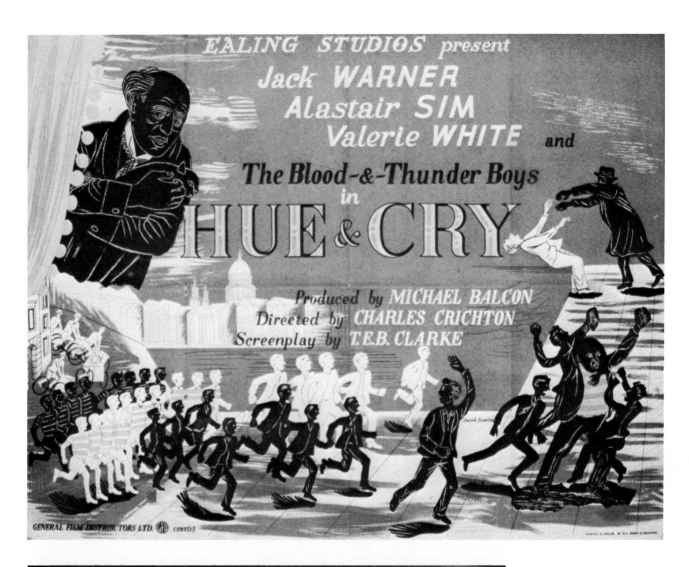

scheming mistress Sibella, whilst he himself is depicted at a gaol window awaiting execution for the one murder he did not commit. Fitton also worked for Frank Pick of London Transport fame, producing posters for the Holborn Empire and Sadlers Wells theatres. He also designed the poster for *Meet Mr Lucifer* (1953), a rather half-hearted attack on television now viewed with a touch of irony, for the BBC took over Ealing Studios only a few years later.

121   Cavalcanti's *Nicholas Nickleby* was another Edwardian film, but was somewhat overshadowed by David Lean's adaptations of Dickens, although Edward Ardizzone's poster was well suited to the subject. James Boswell's colourful style 122 evokes the atmosphere of three highly exciting Ealing dramas: *It Always Rains on* 115 *Sunday* (1947), *The Blue Lamp* (1950) and *The Pool of London* (1951). Boswell also 128 produced the dramatic poster for *The Brave Don't Cry* (1952), about 118 men trapped in a gas-filled mine. This film was produced by Group 3, a unit set up by the British National Film Corporation to foster young talent.

    In 1953 Edward Bawden designed a humorous poster for another piece of Ealing whimsy, *The Titfield Thunderbolt* (1953), the first Ealing comedy in Technicolor, 114 about the campaign by a group of villagers to keep their local branch line open by running the railway themselves.

    Ealing's first venture into Technicolor had been the period romance *Saraband for* 110 *Dead Lovers* (1948), starring Joan Greenwood and Stewart Granger. It told the story of Prince George Louis of Hanover's wife and her affair with Count Koenigsmark, a dashing soldier of fortune, who is assassinated when the truth is discovered. The baroque style of the film is reflected convincingly in Robert Medley's poster.

120   Medley also designed the poster for *Bitter Springs* (1950), the third of the Ealing colonial films, depicting contention over land rights in the 1900s between white settlers and Australian aborigines. This desire to be reminded of colonial history also 114 resulted in Ealing's *Eureka Stockade* (1949), *The Overlanders* (1946), *West of Zanzibar* (1954) and *Where No Vultures Fly* (1951). John Minton designed the posters for *Eureka Stockade* and *Where No Vultures Fly*, both of which are rich in colour with fine detail and bold outlines. A similar style is used for Associated British Pathé's more 128 domestic drama *For Them That Trespass* (1948), directed by Cavalcanti. With other major companies following Ealing's example of poster design, it is evident that Danischewsky's policy was proving worthwhile.

    In 1950 Michael Powell and Emeric Pressburger produced the energetic *The* 127 *Elusive Pimpernel*, starring David Niven. The three-sheet poster, although not using the method, certainly simulates the style of the Beggarstaff Brothers, with large areas of flat colour and almost no detail whatsoever. Associated British also used a simple graphic style to produce the extremely dramatic image of Pinky Brown in Graham 126 Greene's *Brighton Rock* (1947). Group 3 engaged the cartoonist Osbert Lancaster to 119 produce an amusing poster for their comedy *Laxdale Hall* (1952). Another cartoonist, Ronald Searle, created the background drawings for S John Woods' poster of *The* 110 *Lavender Hill Mob* in 1951. This continuation of the Ealing comedies concerned a bullion robbery masterminded by a humble bank clerk. It won an Oscar for screenwriter T. E. B. Clarke and was named the British Film Academy's best film of the year. The central image on the poster is a photograph of the ecstatic 'master criminals', played by Alec Guinness and Stanley Holloway. The following year Searle 124 produced the poster for Associated British Pathé's *Castle in the Air* with Margaret Rutherford, and subsequently went on to create his famous drawings of the St Trinians schoolgirls, adopted in the posters for all the films including the most typical, 124 *Pure Hell of St Trinians* (1960).

104   Other singular posters of the 1950s include those for Laurence Olivier's *Richard* 118 *III* and Stobbs' *A Kid for Two Farthings*, both 1955, for Carol Reed. In 1959 Alec Guinness starred as Joyce Cary's eccentric artist Gulley Jimson in Ronald Neame's

The Lavender Hill Mob
Ronald Searle/S John Woods
30 x 40/76.2 x 101.6
1951

A recurring theme of Ealing comedy — the triumph of the 'little man' over the big battalions of business and bureaucracy — is humorously evoked by a combination of Alec Guinness' and Stanley Holloway's image of rapture against a background of Ronald Searle's unique brand of caricature.

Saraband for Dead Lovers
Robert Medley
30 x 40/76.2 x 101.6
1948

In the 1940s commercial poster designers were well renumerated for their work. Contrarily, film poster designers were generally payed a great deal less. Ealing Studios were the exception to this rule and sustained their policy by paying the appropriate fees. This resulted in an avoidance of colour photo lithography for designs drawn directly onto the plates using anywhere between four to nine colours. A fine example is Robert Medley's *Saraband For Dead Lovers*, a handsomely mounted historical melodrama and Ealing's first film in colour.

The Horse's Mouth. The paintings in the film, created by the artist John Bratby, *118* formed the basis for the film poster designed by Eric Pulford. Pulford, born in 1915, worked as a commercial artist for a process house in Leeds before beginning freelance work for the Rank Organization at the beginning of the 1940s. After the production of his first poster for Thorold Dickinson's *Gaslight* in 1940, Pulford created around 500 designs including those for such distinctive films as *Henry V* (1944), *Odd Man Out* (1947) and *Oliver Twist* (1948), plus all the Norman Wisdom films and most of the *Carry On* series, which began in 1958.

<u>DESIGN AND PRINTING</u>

The design process included first seeing the film, then providing the publicity manager with up to ten rough sketches and subsequently submitting two or three semi-finished designs for approval to the managing director of the film distribution company, the producer and director of the film and any other involved parties. Once approved, Pulford either executed the finished artwork himself or commissioned other artists such as, in the case of *The Horse's Mouth*, the Italian Simbari. Other artists who produced finished art to Pulford's designs included Renatto Fratini for such films as *Waterloo* (1970), *Cromwell* (1970) and *Khartoum* (1966) and more recently Brian Bysouth for *The Golden Voyage of Sinbad* (1973) and Walt Disney films. Pulford returned to the completion of finished art himself for the posters *Breathless* and *The Evil That Men Do*.

The final task in poster design would be to place the work with an appropriate printer. Back in the 1950s the larger theatrical printers were Stafford of Nottingham, Charles Read, The Haycock Press, Lonsdale and Bartholomew and Ripley of London and W. E. Berry of Bradford. At this time the bulk of these printers' work was poster printing, but now at Berry's it comprises around 8% of their business.

Berry's printing history can be dated back to the 1880s. Their history of theatrical paper began with an involvement in McNaughton's well-known vaudeville circuit after the First World War and the printing of film posters became an extension of this. The firm was founded by William Edward Berry, a stereotypical Northern industrialist who knew how to sell and how to spend, often wiring back to his office from his London hotel for 'more cash'. One of his major film clients was Paramount, who generated so much business that an extension to the old printing works was necessary. According to Peter Lee, great-grandson of W. E. Berry and current owner of the firm, 'They always said that Paramount Pictures were paying for the extension basically because of the amount of work they gave us.' Berry's distributed all Paramount's posters, including those printed by other firms, right up to the founding of National Screen Service. The poster artwork was usually sent up to Bradford from London and the key craftsmen would then hand-draw an interpretation of this artwork directly on to the plate. Peter Lee explains:

> 'They had what you'd call the 'black man', he was the key craftsman; he drew the key plate for the black printer and again pulled an impression from that and the 'colour men' rubbed the impression down on to the old plates and drew the colours to the black. The apprentices always started on yellows, as that was the least important colour, yellows and flesh colours.'

The posters were printed on four 40 x 60 machines, which were all placed in a line.

> 'The job literally went – yellow, red, blue, black – along these four machines and we used to refer to them as the yellow machine and the black machine, because these two never changed colour, the yellow for obvious reasons. It's very difficult once you've dirtied the machine to get it clean again. Black obviously is permanently dirty and the red and the blue used to change a bit because you were often printing flesh colours, as a fifth colour, or a dark blue or a purple.'

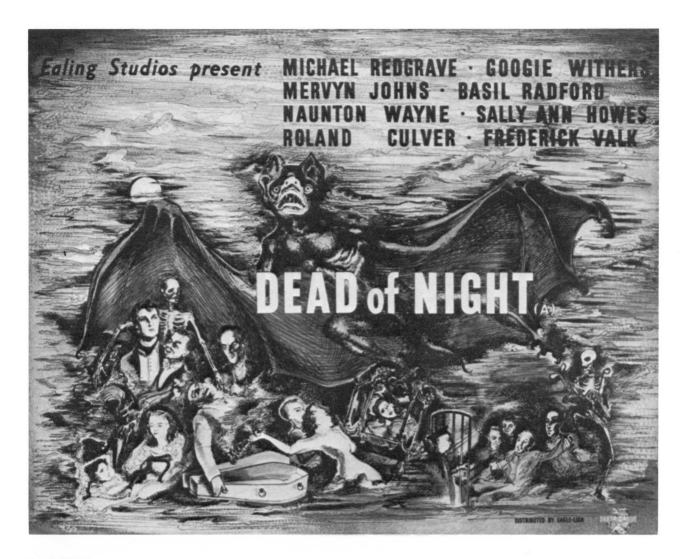

Dead of Night
Leslie Hurry
21½ x 27/55 x 69
1945

Leslie Hurry's
commission to design
the poster for *Dead of
Night* — Ealing Studios'
first post-war film — was
ideally suited to an artist
who, after a great deal of
searching, had found a
perfect outlet for
expressing his
subconscious thoughts
in the settings and
costumes of the Sadler's
Wells ballets *Hamlet* and
Le Lac des Cygnes.

The Titfield Thunderbolt
Edward Bawden
30 x 40/76.2 x 101.6
1953

Edward Bawden had already produced illustrations for the London and North Eastern Railway and many posters for the London Underground. He was therefore no newcomer to the art of the railway when commissioned to design this poster, which is produced in his characteristic style.

Eureka Stockade
John Minton
30 x 40/76.2 x 101.6
1949

John Minton's paintings combined romanticism with the stylistic resources of modern art. His warm colours and knowledge of foliage are evident in all his posters, including *Eureka Stockade*.

Kind Hearts and Coronets
James Fitton
30 x 40/76.2 x 101.6
1949

James Fitton's buoyant style was highly appropriate for capturing the whimsicality and irony of Ealing's most celebrated film, *Kind Hearts and Coronets*.

Pool of London
James Boswell
30 x 40/76.2 x 101.6
1951

A film set around the docks and Tower Bridge areas of London. James Boswell also created posters for the London films *The Blue Lamp* and *It Always Rains on Sunday* (page 120).

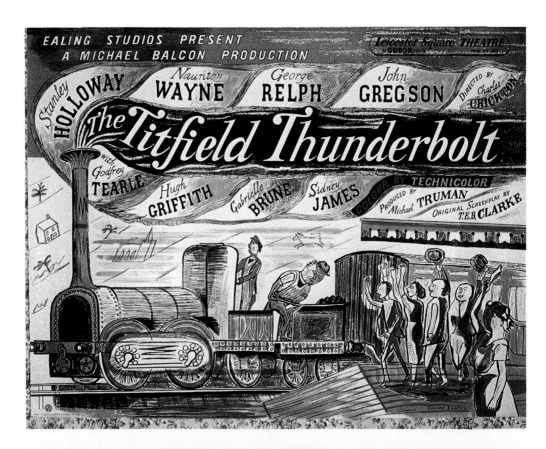

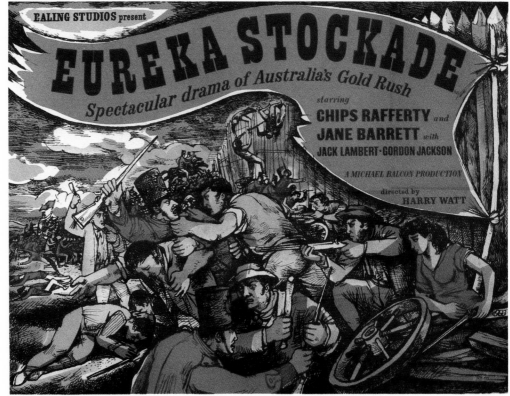

Stone lithography was already being phased out when Berry's began their film trade and direct lithography was used right up to the 1950s, when they finally changed to colour offset printing.

'Direct means straight from the image, transferred to a middle cylinder, which usually carries a rubber blanket, and then onto the paper, and the only reason that offset came in was that you got a better transference of ink from metal to rubber and rubber to paper. You had a better transference that way rather than metal to paper, but direct was used long, long after the rest of the commercial side of the trade had gone onto offset for posters because you could really wallop ink through. There's a limit to how much ink you can transfer from metal to rubber but basically there was no limit to what you could do by the direct method, and so for the solids and the big backgrounds it was still a fabulous process.'

Berry's largest print runs in the 1960s were a phenomenal 20,000 quads for the *Carry On* films. This was far higher than the average run of around 4000–6000 for a circuit release. Lee now considers a good run to be in the region of 2000.

Improved production techniques include electronic scanning, which has superseded half-tone screens as the method of colour separation.

'We scan down on very small sizes and very fine dots and project as you would for the big hoarding posters. Quads were always done at same size. The only thing is, we print on a four-colour press now, all in one pass . . . . You couldn't print a poster that way, you were carrying too much ink. So the ink had to dry before you passed the next one through, and so on. The tragedy is, we've never been more technically capable of churning these things out fast and there's hardly any business any more. The quads used to take two days to print. We now have them done in three hours!'

Of the posters illustrated, W. E. Berry printed Bawden's *Hue and Cry* and Boswell's *The Brave Don't Cry*.

Photography was being used more and more for posters, and although not always successfully, interesting examples include *Saturday Night and Sunday Morning* (1960) for Karel Reisz, the exceptional collage for Michael Powell's *Peeping Tom* (1960) and S John Woods' *The Loneliness of the Long Distance Runner* (1962) for Tony Richardson. Ealing's demise in 1959 saw a general return to a more naturalistic style of graphics.

129
125
129

Champagne Charlie
S John Woods/Eric
Fraser/Barnett
Freedman
28¾ x 39/73 x 99
1944

Many Ealing posters
were created by artists
who had spent some
time working for the
influential Curwen Press,
including John Piper,
Edward Bawden,
Edward Ardizzone and
Barnett Freedman.
Freedman's involvement
in lettering and
typography is evident in
the elaborate title for this
poster designed by S
John Woods. The
following year Freedman
also produced a basically
typographical poster for
Ealing's *Johnny
Frenchman*.
Also at Curwen was E.
McKnight Kauffer,
famous for his London
Underground posters
and the post-Cubist
tempera poster for Fritz
Lang's *Metropolis* in
1926.

Things to Come
Kupfer Sachs
10 x 14¼/25.3 x 36
1936

Zsigo Eiben Schutz and
Kupfer Sachs produced
four highly stylized
posters for this epic
science fiction film,
directed by William
Cameron Menzies. The
illustration here is another
design in the same vein
for the campaign book
cover by Kupfer Sachs.

A Kid For Two Farthings
Stobbs
30 x 40/76.2 x 101.6
1955

Stobbs' extremely colourful poster evokes the atmosphere of this whimsical fairy tale set in Petticoat Lane.

The Horse's Mouth
Eric Pulford
30 x 40/76.2 x 101.6
1959

The film, adapted from a novel by Joyce Carey, revolves around the eccentric artist Gulley Jimson, played by Alec Guinness. One of his eccentricities results in a mural of feet being painted on the wall of an unsuspecting prospective buyer's flat. The mural (actually painted by the artist John Bratby) is reflected in Eric Pulford's poster by two enormous feet.

Laxdale Hall
Osbert Lancaster
30 x 40/76.2 x 101.6
1952

In 1951, the British National Film Finance Corporation set up a unit — called Group 3 — for employing young talent, under the guidance of John Grierson. Also in charge were John Baxter and Michael Balcon and the films produced were typically in the Ealing vein. Not surprisingly, the posters were commissioned in the same manner. *Laxdale Hall* is a comedy about five Hebridean car owners who refuse to pay the road licences until a decent road has been built. The cartoonist Osbert Lancaster illustrates the five car owners in characteristic manner.

Whisky Galore!
Tom Eckersley
30 x 40/76.2 x 101.6
1949

In 1934 Tom Eckersley launched a partnership with Eric Lombers which generated some highly successful graphics for London Transport, the General Post Office, the BBC, Shell Mex and Austin Reed. During the war years they produced posters together and individually for the Ministry of Information and the GPO.

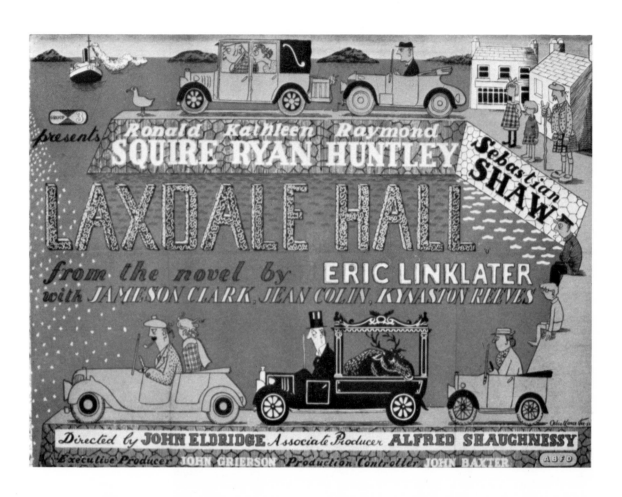

Bitter Springs
Robert Medley
30 x 40/76.2 x 101.6
1950

Medley's pen and ink
washes create a
powerful image for the
third and last of the
robust outdoor
Australian adventures
filmed at Ealing's
Pagewood Studios near
Sydney.

Nicholas Nickleby
Edward Ardizzone
22 x 28/55.9 x 71.1
1947

Edward Ardizzone is best
known for his children's
book illustrations, such
as those for Walter de la
Mare's *Peacock Pie*. His
work, including the
poster for *Nicholas
Nickleby*, which was
drawn directly onto the
lithographic stone, is in
the tradition of
Cruikshank, Charles
Keene and Caldecott
and was well-suited to
this Dickens adaptation.
He also designed the
poster for Ealing's *The
Magnet* in 1950.

The Blue Lamp
James Boswell
30 x 40/76.2 x 101.6
1950

It Always Rains on Sunday
James Boswell
30 x 40/76.2 x 101.6
1947

Atmospheric London locations were the background to some tense Ealing dramas. *It Always Rains on Sunday* takes place in Bethnel Green; *The Blue Lamp*, shot in West London, climaxes in White City Stadium. The New Zealander James Boswell created correspondingly atmospheric posters for each film.

Train of Events
Reginald Mount
30 x 40/76.2 x 101.6
1949

An effective use of vanishing point and lettering for this portmanteau drama revolving around the lives of a number of passengers aboard an express train heading for a crash.

Against the Wind
Manfred Reiss
30 x 40/76.2 x 101.6
1948

A dynamic design was created for this Ealing film about a saboteur training school and a mission to rescue one of their group from a prison in Occupied Belgium.

Castle in the Air
Ronald Searle
30 x 40/76.2 x 101.6
1952

The poor Earl of
Locharne's rich
American cousin vies
with the Coal Board to
purchase his castle,
whilst a genealogist
(played by Margaret
Rutherford, repeating
her cameo role in the
1949 *Passport to
Pimlico*) endeavours to
prove that he is the
rightful heir to the
Scottish throne. It
provides an amusing
situation characterized
by Ronald Searle's
vivacious cartoons.

"Do you know what the most FRIGHTENING thing in the world is...?"

PEEPING TOM

CARL BOEHM
MOIRA SHEARER
ANNA MASSEY
MAXINE AUDLEY

IN EASTMAN COLOUR

Original Story and Screenplay by LEO MARKS

Produced and Directed by MICHAEL POWELL

CERTIFICATE
X
ADULTS ONLY

Distribution by ANGLO AMALGAMATED FILM DISTRIBUTORS LIMITED

The Pure Hell of St Trinian's
Ronald Searle
30 x 40/76.2 x 101.6
1960

This was the third in Frank Launder and Sidney Gilliat's series about the anarchic girls' school of St Trinian's, developed from Ronald Searle's own rakish drawings which first appeared in the 1940s and 50s pin-up magazine *Lilliput*. The drawings of St Trinian's ferocious little female barbarians were originally inspired by the sketches Searle made of his Japanese guards during his time as a prisoner of war. Searle created the posters for all the St Trinian films, along with their credit titles.

Peeping Tom
76.2 x 101.6/30 x 40
1960

The dramatic use of an eye as the basis for the poster design exploits the theme at the heart of one of the most controversial, and brilliant, British films of the post-war period.

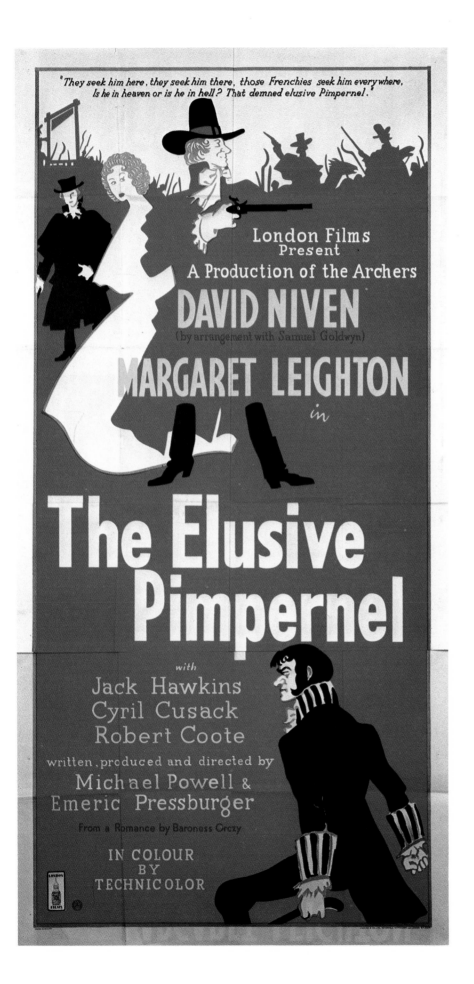

Brighton Rock
27 x 40/68.6 x 101.6
1947

This dramatic image of juvenile gangster Pinky Brown (played by Richard Attenborough) evokes the moody atmosphere of the film, which was shot by Harry Waxman in contrasting black and white and a great deal of shadow.

The Elusive Pimpernel
40 x 80/101.6 x 203.2
1950

The large flat areas of colour and minimal detail in this poster are reminiscent of the designs produced at the turn of the century by the Beggarstaff Brothers.

The Brave Don't Cry
James Boswell
30 x 40/76.2 x 101.6
1952

Boswell's sombre imagery evokes this reconstruction of the Knockshinnock mine disaster when 118 men seemed hopelessly trapped below ground after subsidence and flooding.

For Them That Trespass
30 x 40/76.2 x 101.6
1949

For Them That Trespass was released in the year that Jack Beddington, head of publicity at Shell, praised the Ealing policy in the Penrose Annual. His message may well have penetrated the publicity department at Associated British Pathé, as this poster employs a style not unlike John Minton's *Eureka Stockade* (page 116).

The Loneliness of the Long Distance Runner
S John Woods
30 x 40/76.2 x 101.6
1962

After producing *Saturday Night and Sunday Morning*, Tony Richardson went on to direct *A Taste of Honey* and *The Loneliness of the Long Distance Runner*. The latter, based in a borstal school, shows the institution's star runner, played by Tom Courtenay, deliberately losing a cross-country race as an act of defiance against the authorities. S John Woods exploits Courtenay's defiant mien to great effect.

Saturday Night and Sunday Morning
30 x 40/76.2 x 101.6
1960
Karel Reisz's successful and influential depiction of British working-class life from within is represented by this dramatic poster in which the rebellious Arthur Seaton (played by Albert Finney) provides the central image.

6 THE SPIRIT OF INDEPENDENCE THE ARTIST AS AUTEUR

During the last decade of the 19th century the poster became a major tool of the Industrial Revolution, advances in technology and the arts heralding the advertising poster's coming of age. It did not take long for the expertise gained to be applied to the cinema. Before 1914 France dominated the world film market, with Pathé in particular distributing twice as many films in the United States as all the American companies combined. With this outburst of cinematic activity came a corresponding demand for an industry capable of supplying vast quantities of posters. In response, more and more printing houses and design studios appeared, each founded by, or attracting skilled lithographers and apprentice designers.

If Louis Lumière was the pioneer of the newsreel and documentary film, then George Méliès was the pioneer of fiction and fantasy. Inspired by the Lumières' demonstration at the Grand Café, Méliès' early films were no more than imitations, but he soon began to explore the more imaginative possibilities of the camera. By the turn of the century he had already produced 230 short films, had converted his magic theatre exclusively to the showing of films and had built Europe's first film studio at Montreuil. His experimentation in trick photography culminated in what is probably his most famous film, *Le Voyage dans la Lune* (1902). However, by 1910 the novelty of his trick films began to wane and his fortune dwindled. The poster for his last classic fantasy, *A la Conquête du Pôle* (1912) was designed by Candido Aragonèse de Faria, head of the printing house already contracted to Pathé, who were now distributors of Méliès' films. The film was based on Jules Verne's story *The Sphinx of the Ice-fields*, (1897). A group of explorers are gobbled up by the Giant of the Snows (a huge, studio-bound puppet) and regurgitated, but then find themselves drawn toward, and stuck to, the magnetic pole. Faria's poster depicts the explorers' flying machine over the polar ice cap and is extremely rich in detail and colour, a very rare example of Méliès' pioneering fantasy work.

A la Conquête du Pôle
Candido Aragonèse de Faria
47¼ x 63/120 x 160
1912

Head of his own studio, Faria produced numerous posters for Charles Pathé.

Another pioneering French studio, that of Charles Pathé at Vincennes, employed 1500 staff by 1908 and his production companies, which had been set up all over the world, produced such a vast quantity of films that it was necessary to use many other printing houses and studios to manufacture the necessary posters. Daniel de Losques had produced illustrations for the satirical magazine *Le Rire* after leaving a career in law and administration, and set up his own graphic studio, Affiches de Losques, in 1910, producing posters for the music hall and particularly Mistinguett. His experience in caricature enabled him to create some jovial posters for Pathé's star comedians, Max Linder and Prince Rigadin.

<u>HEROES AND VILLAINS</u>

Ferdinand Zecca began directing films for Pathé in 1901. More of a businessman than Méliès, he exploited the commercial potential of the medium, and although somewhat of a plagiarist, did introduce the lower-class crime melodrama to the cinema in such films as *Histoire d'un Crime* (1901), *Les Victimes de l'Alcoolisme* (1902) and *La Grève* (1904). Zecca collaborated with the designer V. Lorant-Heilbronn, a student of Georges-Antoine Rochegrosse, who produced several posters for the Chatelet theatre, the theatre of varieties and the Café Concerts from his own studio. He designed a vividly dramatic poster for Zecca's *La Grève*, which was printed by Faria, and produced many other fine posters for Pathé.

Zecca's heir in creating low-life crime films was Louis Feuillade, who began working for Gaumont in 1906, producing a series of comedies with the child stars Bébé and later Bout-de-Zou. He then brought into the crime film an element of fantasy, with master criminals and masked avengers, the first being the hooded Fantômas in a series made in 1913. Its popularity was such that it was followed in 1915–16 by the two-part demi-serial *Les Vampires*, the twelve-episode serial *Judex*, the caped avenger in 1916, *La nouvelle mission de Judex* in 1917 and *Tih Minh* in 1918.

The film companies were fully aware of the importance of the poster designer and used professionals to design posters for what they considered their better films. The prolific artist Achille Luciano Mauzan produced many paintings and caricatures, several thousand postcards and around 6000 posters including a singularly fine one for *Les Vampires*. The Italian Leonetto Cappiello began to make a name for himself in Paris, around 1900. His designs were derived from the earlier pioneers such as Chéret, but were simplified and expressed the change from the leisurely 'Belle Epoque' to the faster age of the automobile. He rarely ventured into cinema, but was requested by Feuillade to produce a two-panel (160 x 240) poster for his *Judex*, which depicts the caped avenger threatening his next victim via some bizarre electrical contrivance. The Spanish portrait painter Emilio Vilà, who specialized in extremely fine stone lithographs of cinema stars (including William S. Hart and Maria Felix) was commissioned to design a poster for *Tih Minh*.

Imitations and successors of the super-villain and super-hero prevailed. The unsigned poster for *Maciste Contre Tous* is from the 1920s. Maciste first appeared as the hero in the Italian film *Cabiria* (1913). Another unsigned poster from the 1920s is *Un Vrai Bandit*, derived from an American import of 1926, *The Social Highwayman*, starring John Patrick as an intrepid junior reporter tracking down a local bandit. The poster image is taken directly from a studio production still.

<u>THE ART FILM AND THE IMPRESSIONISTS</u>

In the 1920s the critic Louis Delluc played an important role in the founding of cinema clubs and elevating the status of cinema as an art. Influenced by such American films as De Mille's *The Cheat* (1915), he began to experiment with films where atmosphere transcended plot, which in some cases was actually non-existent. Under Delluc's

134

135

influence, the young Jean Epstein produced his first film, the documentary *Pasteur*, and in 1926 was assisted by Luis Buñuel on the film *Mauprat*. The poster for this was designed by Boris Bilinsky, a Ukrainian who came to Paris in 1922 and produced exotic scenery for the theatre and ballet. He became associated with the colony of Russian emigrés in Paris, including Leon Bakst, and began working in the cinema, producing costumes for Jean Epstein's *Lions des Mogols* (1924) and contributing to the scenery for Fritz Lang's *Metropolis* in 1927.

138

Prominent amongst these Impressionist film-makers was Marcel l'Herbier, who in 1924 produced the experimental avant-garde film *L'Inhumaine*. The unrestrained narrative was in the style of earlier Danish and Italian experimental films, with Georgette Leblanc playing a super-vamp. L'Herbier gathered together a host of contemporary talents, including the supreme Art Deco architect Robert Mallet-Stevens who designed the Art Deco sets, Darius Milhaud who provided the music, and the controversial painter Fernand Léger who designed the Cubo-Futurist laboratory setting which is echoed in the poster by Djo Bourgeois. The poster for L'Herbier's subsequent film of 1925, *Feu Mathias Pascal*, was produced by Alain Cuny, who began his acting career in the 1930s, started work in the French cinema as a costume and set designer for Cavalcanti, Feyder and Renoir and produced a fine collection of film posters in the 1920s.

The luminary of the Impressionist school was Abel Gance, who began writing scripts for Gaumont in 1909 and directing in 1911. In 1923 he started work on his monumental *Napoléon*, which not only included all the known innovations in film technique, but much more besides. Parts of the action were shot by three cameras simultaneously, to produce a triptych effect which anticipated the Cinerama process by thirty years. The subjective camera work was phenomenal. In the Corsican chase sequence, one camera was strapped to a galloping horse; another in a waterproof box was dropped into the Mediterranean from the cliff-tops to convey the imagery seen by Napoleon in his own dive; and yet another was strapped to a singer's breast to record the rhythm of the *Marseillaise*. The original film poster for *Napoléon* was designed by Tamagno (a celebrated circus poster designer who also produced a poster for the 1920s war film *Verdun Tel Que Poilu l'a Vécu . . . .*); the sheet illustrated on page 140 is that which accompanied the reissue of *Napoléon* in 1950 and was designed by the Italian Duccio-Marvasi.

136
140

One of the great French film poster designers was Jean-Albert Mercier. Born in 1899, he was a student of the Ecole des Beaux Arts in Angers and the Ecole Nationale des Arts Décoratifs in Paris, in 1922. Hundreds of film posters followed his first design for Jean Epstein's *Les Aventures de Robert Macaire* in 1925. A very fine first poster, portraying Jean Angelo as Robert Macaire, it used broad areas of bright colour. Mercier produced another poster for Epstein's *Mauprat*, in a similar style, and again for Epstein's *Six et Demi-Onze* of 1927. In 1930 Abel Gance produced *La Fin du Monde*, for which Mercier designed two different posters, both using flat areas of variegated tone. In 1931 he created a startling work for *Fantômas*, directed by Paul Fejos, in which the image consists entirely of two huge luminous, bloodshot eyes. The irises are emerald green, and surrounding the eyes is a turquoise luminescence against a black background. Light reflections on the eyes are of the same lime green as the simple title, which spans the bottom of the two-panel poster.

TRANSITION TO SOUND

In 1927 Mercier had produced another dynamic poster, of an automobile chase, for René Clair's *La Proie du Vent*. René Clair came into his own with the arrival of sound, which, ironically, he had originally opposed. He realized the potential that natural sound and music could bring to film, however, and embarked on the production of four of the most imaginative films produced in this transition period: *Sous les Toits de*

Maciste contre Tous
47¼ x 63/120 x 160
c. 1920

Maciste was one of
several popular super
heroes who flourished in
the cinema of the time.

Un Vrai Bandit
31½ x 47¼/80 x 120
1926

The heavy outline was a
popular device in the
1920s.

Paris (1930), *Le Million* and *A Nous la Liberté* (1931) and *14 Juillet* (1932). Mercier produced posters for each of the last three films, the most successful being *14 Juillet*, which evokes the spirit of French national celebration with crowded squares, dancing, lanterns, fireworks and accordions — all effectively conveyed in Mercier's poster. Mercier continued to produce posters for the major film-makers up till the outbreak of war.

Marcel Pagnol used the change-over to sound to preserve important plays on film, much to the horror of the critics. Small wonder then that his first two films, *Marius* in 1931 and *Fanny* in 1932, from his own plays, were indignantly received. The intelligent acting and atmospheric Marseilles location work appealed to the public, however, and along with *César* in 1936, they form a nostalgic tribute to the Provençal way of life. *César*, played by Raimu, runs a bar, where he drinks pastis and cheats at cards. He is dedicated to his son Marius, played by Pierre Fresnay, who is torn between two loves, Fanny, played by Orane Demazis (Pagnol's wife), and the sea. Marius breaks his father's heart when he sleeps with Fanny and, not knowing that she has become pregnant, goes off to sea. César's friend Panisse also loves Fanny; happy to stand as father to the child, he marries her. When Marius returns and realizes that the child is his, César persuades him to leave again. Twenty years pass and Panisse dies. Césariot, the son, is shattered when he discovers the story and traces Marius to a garage in Toulon. As a joke, Césariot is told that Marius is a smuggler, which infuriates César when he hears of it, but when the truth is learnt, all are finally united. The great cartoonist Albert Dubout produced the three posters for the trilogy at Pagnol's request.

Marcel Pagnol's publicity director between 1930 and 1940 was André Toé, and he produced various posters in a caricature style imbued with Art Deco. Typical is *Le Schpountz* of 1938, a social satire starring Fernandel as a janitor who has aspirations for the high life. A more solid caricature style was employed by Henri Cerutti, who also designed posters for Pagnol. Cerutti came from a family of lithographers and had an early interest in cartoons before beginning as a film poster designer at the age of 18, following a career which he continued till 1968. He also designed a very fine poster for Jean Vigo's *L'Atalante* in 1934.

Jean Renoir began making films in the 1920s and started to achieve considerable commercial and artistic success after the advent of sound. One of his earliest sound films was *La Nuit du Carrefour* in 1932, a mysterious adaptation of a Georges Simenon novel, with Pierre Renoir as Inspector Maigret. The aura conveyed by Jean Bertrand's poster reflects Renoir's idea of subordinating plot to atmosphere which, according to the director, in a sense succeeded: 'in the matter of mystery the result exceeded our expectation, particularly since, two reels having been lost, the story was pretty well incomprehensible, even to its author.'

Another adaptation was *Les Bas-Fonds*, directed by Renoir in 1936 and taken from a Gorky play which, according to the playwright, involved nothing but atmosphere. The portrayal of a disgraced nobleman's descent into the 'lower depths' was seen as a mixture of realism, tragedy and burlesque. Jean-René Poissonnié highlights the poster for *Les Bas-Fonds* with the image of Jean Gabin, who plays the thief determined to climb out of the 'lower depths'. Poissonnié was a versatile member of the 1945 Syndicate for Film Poster Designers, which was formed by another renowned poster designer, Edgard Derouet. His emblem of the bow and pencil appears on many post-war posters.

Yet another Renoir adaptation was *La Bête Humaine* (1938), a melodrama based on a novel by Zola, with superb acting by Jean Gabin and Simone Simon cast deliberately against type. The film uses powerful rhythmic editing with its opening and closing railway journeys filmed from the footplate of the engine. Renoir also experimented with depth of field, particularly in the murder scene, where the man and

Verdun (*tel que poliu l'a vécu . . . .*)
Tamagno
31½ x 47¼/80 x 120
c. 1920

Malclé's surrealistic style evokes the poetic atmosphere of Jean Cocteau's enchanting fantasy.

L'Inhumaine
Djo Bourgeois
47¼ x 63/120 x 160
1924

The design of Djo
Bourgeois' poster is
derived from the film's
laboratory setting
created by the Cubist,
Fernand Leger.

Les Bas-Fonds
Jean-René Poissonnié
1936

Poissonnié poster
emphasizes Jean
Gabin's image of 'the
tragic hero of
contemporary cinema'.

14 Juillet
Jean-Albert Mercier
47¼ x 63/120 x 160
1932

Mercier's finest film
posters were produced
for the Impressionist film
school, particularly for
René Clair and his *14
Juillet*.

La Bête Humaine
63 x 94½/160 x 240
1938

Individual design has
been substituted here by
extreme Hollywood
influences.

Napoléon
Duccio-Marvasi
47¼ x 63/120 x 160

This poster for the 1950
re-release of *Napoléon*
was produced by the
Italian designer Duccio-
Marvasi.

140 woman stand out against a completely blurred background. The poster for *La Bête Humaine*, which is unsigned, is a prime example of the strong Hollywood influences prevalent at this time.

EFFECTS OF THE GERMAN OCCUPATION

The outbreak of war and subsequent Occupation shattered the French film industry. Renoir, Clair and Duvivier had gone to Hollywood, and Jacques Feyder had taken refuge in Switzerland. As Minister of Public Enlightenment and Propaganda, Goebbels controlled all film production, which had to be submitted to the scrutiny of two censors, the German *Propagandastaffel* and that of the Vichy government. The one major film-maker left in Paris was Marcel Carné, who managed to avoid direct confrontation with authority by placing his films out of the present time, and, in complete contrast to the realism practised by the pre-war school, absorbed himself in fantasy. The initial result was the brilliant *Les Visiteurs du Soir*, released in 1942 to an enthusiastic public. The story is set in a castle in the Middle Ages to which the devil sends emissaries with the task of disrupting a courtly wedding, but is unable to change the course of true love. It is a seemingly symbolical tale of Hitler's inability to
148 break the national spirit. The unsigned poster assembles the protagonists in a border derived from medieval book illumination.

The crowning achievement of the Occupation period was Carné's *Les Enfants du Paradis*, released in 1945. This was the most sumptuous film produced by the team of Marcel Carné and screenwriter Jacques Prévert, using the romantic styles of comic parody, dramatic mime, melodrama and tragedy to relate a story of the impossibility of love in an ill-conceived world, a world of the popular stage and the
151 underworld of Paris in the 1840s. Jacques Bonneaud's poster describes the cast of the film in an elegantly designed composition: the warm-hearted mime artist, Debureau, played by Jean-Louis Barrault, in and out of make-up; the courtesan who sacrifices love for money, played by Arletty; the up and coming actor and courtesan's former lover Lemaître, played by Pierre Brasseur; the devoted wife Nathalie, outwardly gentle but fanatically religious, played by Maria Casares; the intellectual anarchist and murderer, Lacenaire, played by Marcel Herrand; the wealthy nobleman played by Louis Salou and the evil old-clothes man played by Pierre Renoir. The background scene, taken from a still of the film in reverse, shows the audience, the gallery gods, the 'children of paradise' at the famous Funambules theatre in Paris, demanding that the performance, the action of the film, should continue.

Jacques Bonneaud, born in 1898, was a student at the Ecole de la Place des Vosges and the Ecole B. Palissy. He won first prize for the general competition in design in Paris in 1916 and after working in the Cormon studio at the Ecole des Beaux Arts, took his apprenticeship at Faria's printing house. In a period of around thirty years he produced more than 2000 posters for films by Duvivier, Renoir, Carné, Clouzot, Guitry and other leading film-makers.

151 An alternative poster for *Les Enfants du Paradis*, that produced by Georges Allard for the publicity agent J. Fourastié, depicts Nathalie and Debureau, who are now married and both successful, but with Debureau, still in love with the courtesan
150 Garance, attempting to avoid Nathalie's attention. Bernard Lancy's poster for the same film depicts the fight between Debureau and Lacenaire's confederate bully. Lancy was a major film poster designer who began his long and brilliant career in 1921 with a design for a Louis Feuillade serial, and then produced over 100 posters up till 1950. His fine compositions for some of the classics of French cinema included a superb design for Renoir's *La Grande Illusion* (1937). Recognized by his colleagues as a master, he became President of Honour of the Syndicate of 1945. Many posters originating at the studio which he owned and headed were signed 'at. B. Lancy', including the dramatic poster for Paul Mesnier's *La Kermesse Rouge*.

La Nuit du Carrefour
Jean Bertrand
47¼ x 63/120 x 160
1932

The effect conveyed by Bertrand's poster reflects Jean Renoir's desire to sustain atmosphere, even at the expense of the film's plot.

Le Schpountz
André Toé
23½ x 31½/60 x 80
1937

Toé was well-known for his poster portraits of film stars Raimu and Fernandel, drawn in the Art Deco style.

Another director who remained in France during the Occupation was Christian-Jacque, who directed *Sortilèges* in 1944, for which Jean Colin executed a most   *152*
unusual poster. Colin was a professional commercial poster designer, but in his long career produced only ten designs for the cinema, including that for the first French release of Jean Vigo's *Zéro de Conduite* in 1945.

POST-WAR REALISM

The post-war realist trend owed more to the fatalistic films of Renoir and Carné in the 1930s than to the contemporary reality underlying Italian Neo-realism. René Clément's *Les Maudits* of 1946 is a story of Nazis and collaborators aboard a submarine wandering in the Atlantic after the fall of Berlin. In René Péron's poster the tortured figures convey the fear and madness visualized at the climax of the film. René Péron was one of the most prolific and skilful film poster designers, producing more than 2000 posters from the 1920s to the late 1950s. Then from the 1960s onwards he devoted his time to the illustration of children's books. In 1954 he created a poster for Jean Renoir's *French Cancan*, a spirited and sentimental story of the founding of the   *153*
Moulin Rouge at the height of the Belle Epoque. The bright pink, red and blues in Péron's poster recall the gaiety and warmth of this period and the Impressionist paintings of Renoir's father.

Jean Cocteau began his post-war film work in his own individual style with *La Belle et la Bête* (1946), a haunting fantasy adapted from Madame Leprince de Beaumont's fairy tale. The film was full of visual imagery and poetic expression, captured effectively by Jean-Denis Malclé's poster. Malclé was a renowned theatrical   *154*
designer and illustrator, whose occasional film posters, produced in a romantic and surrealistic manner, were highly successful.

In 1950 the influential Paul Colin designed a poster for Robert Bresson's *Journal d'un Curé de Compagne*. Colin was at his peak in the 1920s and 1930s, particularly with his posters for the *Revue Nègre* with Josephine Baker. He borrowed elements from Cubism, the Bauhaus and Art Deco and, with an economic use of colour, created a vast collection of posters with dynamic primary images. At the end of the war, Colin's Liberation poster was plastered all over Paris by the resistance movement. He made rare incursions into cinema, which is all the more provoking considering that a minority of these posters are for equally rare films by Robert Bresson. Bresson's emphasis on flat composition is reiterated by broad areas of uniform colour in Colin's poster. The *Journal d'un Curé de Compagne* is an intense   *155*
and relentless study of a dying priest coming to terms with the notion of a world without God. Colin also produced a similarly dramatic poster for Bresson's *Un Condamné à Mort s'est Echappé* in 1956. The account of a condemned man's escape from prison is symbolized by the simple design of the escape rope hanging over the prison wall.

The humorous side of life was encapsulated in the films of Jacques Tati whose familiar character of Monsieur Hulot, introduced in *Les Vacances de Mr Hulot* (1951), subsequently tries to cope with the new-fangled gadgetry at his brother-in-law's home in *Mon Oncle*, made in 1958. Pierre Etaix's poster perfectly represents Mr   *153*
Hulot's characteristic stance in a simple caricature outline. Etaix was Tati's assistant and gagman on *Mon Oncle* and began directing and starring in his own comedies in 1961. The previous year Jean Cocteau directed his last autobiographical film, *La Testament D'Orphée*, which was probably the most intensely personal of all his   *159*
works. He reworked his drawings of *Saint Orphée martyr de la poésie et de la musique* for the poster of this film.

'La nouvelle vague' emerged in the late 1950s with an explosion of radical activity by young film-makers such as Claude Chabrol, Jean-Luc Godard and François Truffaut and films such as *Les Cousins, A Bout de Souffle* and *Les Quatre*

Cent Coups (1959). In 1968 Truffaut directed *La Mariée Etait en Noir*, an adaptation of Cornell Woolrich's 1940 suspense novel, *The Bride Wore Black*. Julie Kohler, whose husband was accidentally killed on the church steps moments after their wedding, spends years tracking down and systematically murdering the five men she holds responsible. René Ferraci depicts Jeanne Moreau as the bride.

FRENCH DESIGNERS

The posters of French cinema are characterized by their variety of style and approach. In part this is attributable to the numerous artists whose skills have been drawn upon, for many well-known artists and designers, other than those mentioned above, produced posters for the French cinema, either as full-time professionals or on special commissions. The following list includes some of the most notable. Significant film titles, dates, directors and, in some cases, stars, are also given.

Belinsky, Constantin
One of the rare poster designers whose career spans four decades, beginning in the 1930s.
J'Accuse 1937 Abel Gance
Venus aveugle 1941 Abel Gance
Knock 1950 with Louis Jouvet

Bonoit-Levy, J. 1888–1959
He entered the cinema in 1910 and from 1920 directed and produced hundreds of information and educational films. The art director for Jean Epstein's first film, *Pasteur* (1922), he is most famous for his feature films including *La Maternelle* (1933).
Les Trois Mousquetaires 1921 Henri Diamant-Berger

Bucher-Crosmieres, Huguette
Studied at the Ecole des Beaux Arts, then spent two years in the studio of Paul Colin and finally one year with the modern art theoretician, André Lhote. She produced a fine poster for the Cannes Festival plus a series of film posters.
Occupe-toi d'Amélie 1949 Claude Autant-Lara

Carlu, Jean born 1900
A major poster artist who began work in 1917 and was given a retrospective exhibition at the Musée de l'Affiche in 1981. He produced very few film posters, but they are extremely striking and individual.
Le Gosse (French release for *The Kid*) 1922 Charlie Chaplin
Les 4 Plumes Blanches (*The Four Feathers* 1930) 1929 Merian C. Cooper, Ernest Schoedsack
L'Atlantide 1932 G. W. Pabst

Cartier, Roger
One of the few poster caricaturists, he began working in the 1920s.
Le Studio en folie 1951 with Bourvil
Vous n'avez rien à Déclarer 1938 with Raimu

Dreville, Jean born 1906
A former journalist, producing a report on the shooting of Marcel L'Herbier's film, *L'Argent*, he created some extremely original film posters before commencing his career as a film director with the short *Autour de l'Argent* in 1928.
A qui la faute? 1924 with Elizabeth Bergner
L'Escale 1927 Jean Gourguet
Folies de Printemps 1927

Folon, Jean-Michel born 1934
Inolved in all aspects of film, he has produced many very individual posters, including some fine examples for the Cannes Film Festival.
Lily aime-moi 1975 Maurice Dugowson
Solaris 1972 Andrei Tarkovsky

François, Fernand
A designer who produced film posters in a style specifically for Fernandel. He was a member of the Syndicate of 1945.
Fernandel 1939
Forfaiture 1937 Marcel L'Herbier

Gerard, Michel
He produced around twenty posters for the cinema after the Second World War.
L'aigle à deux Têtes 1947 Jean Cocteau
Le Salaire de la Peur 1953 Henri-Georges Clouzot

Gid, Raymond born 1905
A commercial poster designer who trained at the School of Architecture. His film posters were executed in close collaboration with the film producers. Later he became more involved in illustration and typography and participated in world-wide group exhibitions. In 1979 the Bernein-Jeune gallery held a retrospective exhibition of his works.
Vampyr 1932 Carl Dreyer
Les Histoires Extraordinaires R. Oswald
Le Silence du mer 1947 Jean Pierre Melville
La Marie du port 1949 Marcel Carné
Les Diaboliques 1954 Henri-Georges Clouzot
Le Dossier noir 1955 André Cayatte

Giscard, Henry born 1895
A painter who produced a series of posters for Jean Renoir.
Le Tournoi 1929 Jean Renoir

Gray, Henri 1858–1924
He produced numerous lithographs for the theatre, opera, circus and early cinema.
Au Zambèze 1908 for Pathé Frères

Grinsson, Boris born 1907
After Grinsson left Hitler's Germany for France in 1936 he produced several hundred film posters. The bulk of these designs were for French releases of American films and all are produced in a realistic vein, typical of the American posters themselves.
Le Poison (The Lost Weekend) 1945 Billy Wilder
7 Ans de Réflexion (The Seven Year Itch) 1956 Billy Wilder, with Marilyn Monroe
Gilda 1946 with Rita Hayworth

Guillaume, Albert 1873–1942
An Art Nouveau poster designer who produced designs for the dances of the Elysée-Montmartre and the parties at the Scala.
Exposition de 1900 – Théâtre des bonshommes Guillaume 1900

Marius
Albert Dubout
47¼ x 63/120 x 160
1931

Fanny
Albert Dubout
31½ x 47¼/80 x 120
1932

César
Albert Dubout
31½ x 47¼/80 x 120
1936

Albert Dubout, who died in 1977, created over a hundred humorous film posters in his characteristically colourful, caricature style.

Les Visiteurs du Soir
63 x 94½/160 x 240
1942

A traditional design for
Carné's haunting
fantasy, which provided
an oblique allegory for
the Nazi occupation of
France.

Les Maudits
René Peron
23½ x 31½/60 x 80
1946

In his fifty-year career,
Péron produced over
2,000 posters for the
cinema.

La Kermesse Rouge
At. B. Lancy
47¼ x 63/120 x 160

Posters produced by
other designers at
Lancy's own studio were
signed 'at. B. Lancy'.

Harfort 1898–1973
A printer who designed many posters for the cinema, especially comedies.
Michel Simon 1937 (poster portrait)

Jacquelin, Jean born 1905
Trained at the Ecole Germain Pilon and the Arts Decoratifs, he went into advertising with a particular interest in automobile trademarks. After the war, it was at the request of Jean Mounier that he produced some posters and so began his brilliant career.
Dédée d'Anvers 1947 Yves Allegret
Rocambole 1947
Jour de Fête 1949 Jacques Tati
Les Amants de Vérone 1948 André Cayatte
Casque d'Or 1951 Jacques Becker

Jeanne, Marcel
Trained in lithography, Jeanne was put in charge of the photogravure studio at the Bedos printing house. He created a personal style by combining the two techniques.
Les Frères Bouquinquant 1946 Louis Daquin
Fanfan la Tulipe 1951 Christian-Jacque

Jorio, Albert
Director of the Monegasque printing house at Monte Carlo, he produced many posters including several for Marcel Pagnol.
La Fille du Puisatier 1946 Marcel Pagnol

Labisse, Félix 1905–1982
This surrealist painter, close to Magritte, produced a few film posters.
Le Passe Muraille 1951 Jean Boyer

Lefebvre, René 1914–1975
Director of publicity for Universal for several years and head of his own studio.
Le Diable au Corps 1946 Claude Autant-Lara

Levet, P.
An extremely active designer, producing posters for American and French companies.
Lettres de Mon Moulin 1954 Marcel Pagnol

Mariani
He produced some fine film posters in the 1930s.
Le Parfum de la Dame en Noir 1931 Marcel L'Herbier
Boudu Sauvé des Eaux 1932 Jean Renoir
Drôle de Drame 1937 Marcel Carné

Mascii, Jean born 1926
He produced many posters for American Westerns and spectacles of the 1950s. His finely-detailed designs have become very popular, particularly in the posters for Jean-Paul Belmondo.
Les Yeux sans visage Georges Franju
La Belle de Cadix 1953 Raymond Bernard
Le Bon, le Brut et la Truand Clint Eastwood
Alphaville Jean-Luc Godard

Morvan, Hervé 1917–1980
Advertising poster designer who began producing film posters in 1942; they now form the majority of the 800 or so posters he produced.
L'Aigle à Deux Têtes 1948 Jean Cocteau
Miquette et sa Mère 1950 Henri-Georges Clouzot

Noel, Guy-Gerard
He produced posters for the Pathé Marconi artists of the 1930, including Josephine Baker, and began designing film posters just before the war, producing around 100.
Le Rosier de Madame Husson 1951 Marcel Pagnol
Narcisse Noir (French release of *Black Narcissus*) 1948 Michael Powell

Orazi, Manuel-Joseph Raphaël 1860–1934
Painter, illustrator and master lithographer whose subjects were marked by an exotic symbolism.
L'Atlantide 1921 Jacques Feyder

Pean, René born 1875
A talented student of Chéret and poster designer of the Belle Epoque, producing numerous lithographs for the Chaix printing house. These included posters for the Folies-Bergère, the Moulin de la Galette, the Moulin Rouge and the Universal Exhibition of 1900.
Le Monde Animé l'Aléthorama 1896
The Royal Biograph 1898
L'Univers présenté par les Films 1908

Peynet, Raymond
The cinema rarely used cartoonists to produce posters, but Peynet's amorous cartoons were ideally suited to the films they represented.
La Maternelle 1948 Henri Diamant-Berger
Le Trésor des Pieds Nickelés 1949 Marcel Aboulker

Pigeot, Pierre
A poster designer whose career spread from 1920 to 1950, during which time he produced five or six posters per month. He was commissioned not only by the directors of publicity, but also by the producers and even the actors themselves.
A bas les Hommes 1928 a German film by Georg Jacoby
L'aventure de Cabassou 1946 Fernandel
Le Chanteur Inconnu 1946 Henri Diamant-Berger
Les Portes de la Nuit 1948 Marcel Carné

Rabier, Benjamin 1864–1939
The creator of the Gedeon character, he produced posters for his nine animated films between 1920 and 1922.
Les Amours d'un Escargot 1922 Benjamin Rabier

Roberty
A prolific film poster designer who specialized in a broad, humorous style.
Nièces Espiègles c. 1915
Fatty Pêche (French release of *A Country Hero* 1917) Fatty Arbuckle

Rojac, Roger
Although he executed his own posters, Rojac is better known for his services to the Syndicate.
Antoine et Antoinette 1947 Jacques Becker
Douce 1947 Claude Autant-Lara
Occupe-toi d'Amélie 1949 Claude Autant-Lara

Savignac, Raymond
A poster designer well-known for his post-war work. Winner of the Martini Medaille d'Or in 1964, his posters are characterized by their humour and simple style.
Les Copains 1964 Yves Robert

Soubie, Roger born 1898
Soubie began designing posters in 1924 and continued to produce fine examples, characterized by a subtle use of chiaroscuro, over 1000 all told, until his retirement in 1972.
Trois Balles dans le Pean 1933 Jean Angelo
Domino Noir 1929 with the German actor Harry Liedtke
Tabou 1932 F. W. Murnau
Dr Jekyll et Mr Hyde 1946 with Spencer Tracy and Ingrid Bergman

Villemot, Bernard born 1911
A student of Paul Colin. One of the great poster designers, he was insufficiently used by the cinema industry.
Nous Sommes tous des Assassins 1952 André Cyatte
La Tête contre les Murs 1959

Les Enfants du Paradis
Bernard Lancy
47¼ x 63/120 x 160
1944

A major film posterist, Lancy became head of the Syndicate of Poster Designers in 1945. He produced posters for many other French classics including *La Kermesse Heroique*, *Le Jour se Leve* and *La Grande Illusion*.

Les Enfants du Paradis
Jacques Bonneaud
63 x 94½/160 x 240
1944

A prolific film poster designer, Jacques Bonneaud's elegant and figurative design is an exemplary advertisement for what is still regarded as the finest French film ever made.

Les Enfants du Paradis
George Allard
47½ x 63/120 x 160
1944

George Allard produced many posters for the publicity agent J. Fourastié.

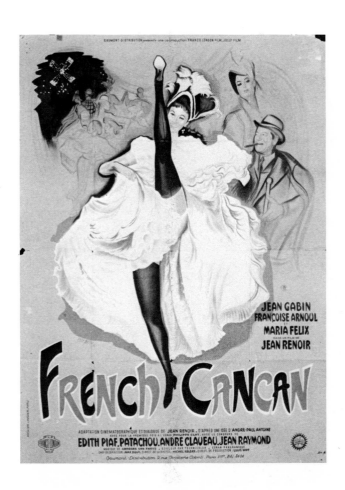

Sortilèges
Jean Colin
47¼ x 63/120 x 160
1944

One of ten film posters
designed by Jean Colin,
who won the Martini
Medaille d'Or in 1960
and the Prix National de
l'Affiche in 1970.

French Cancan
René Peron
45¼ x 64¼/115 x 160.6
1954

Mon Oncle
Pierre Etaix
23½ x 31½/60 x 80
1958

A comedian himself,
Etaix was Tati's gagman
on this film, a mournfully
elegant assault on the
fatuities of modern urban
life.

La Belle et la Bête
Jean-Denis Malclé
47¼ x 63/120 x 160
1946

Malclé's surrealistic style evokes the poetic atmosphere of Jean Cocteau's enchanting fantasy.

Journal d'un Curé de Campagne
Paul Colin
47¼ x 63/120 x 160
1950

Born in Nancy in 1892, Paul Colin started life as a painter, but in 1925 he joined the Théâtre des Champs-Elysées as a stage designer and poster artist, subsequently producing an estimated 2,000 posters. All display an economy of colour and brushstrokes in a most distinctive and recognizable style.

La Mariée était en Noir
René Ferraci
23½ x 31½/60 x 80
1968

Ferraci began designing posters in the mid-1950s, including a memorable work for Jean Renoir's *Elena et les hommes*. His graphic style established him as a leading contemporary film poster designer.

Le Testament d'Orphée
Jean Cocteau
47¼ x 63/120 x 160
1960

Poet, philosopher, dramatist, painter, novelist, set designer, film-maker, script writer and actor, for his last cinematic venture Jean Cocteau was also film poster designer.

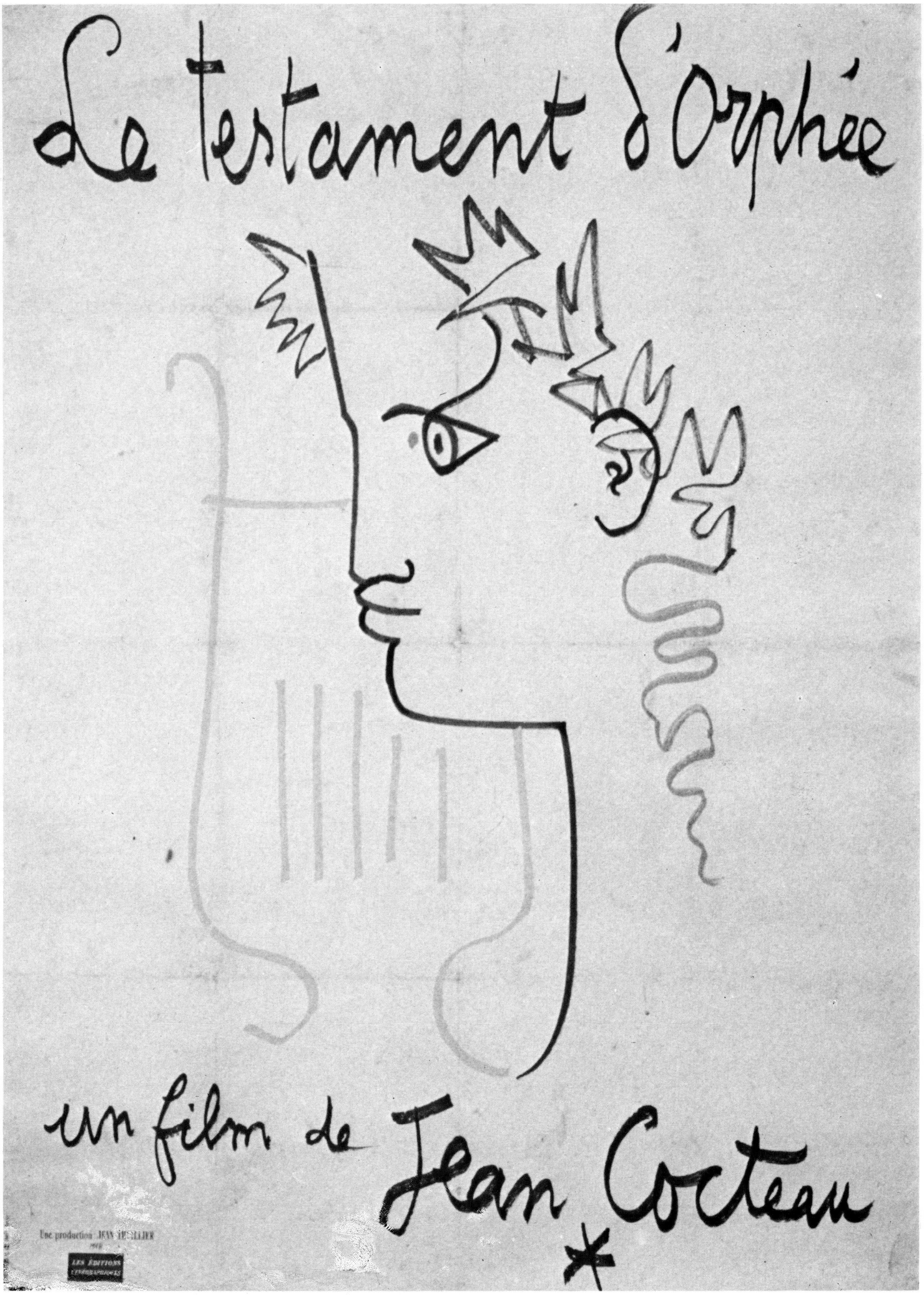
Le testament d'Orphée
un film de Jean Cocteau

7 ART AND LIBERATION
REALISM AND ROMANTICISM IN POLAND AND ITALY

Two outstanding artistic styles emerged in European cinema after the liberation of countries from Nazi Occupation: Italian Neo-realism and the highly individual school of Polish film poster design. In Poland the pre-war cinema industry had existed against a national background of territorial disputes and in such an unstable political climate was technically inefficient and of little interest internationally. Conversely, pre-war posters had achieved moderate success with Adam Baubelski, Tadeusz Gronowski, Jan Mucharski, Tadeusz Trepkowski and Henryk Tomaszewski all producing striking commercial designs. The Polish Workers' Party assumed power not long after the liberation and the cinema was then ruled by the strict dogmas of Socialist Realism. The poster designers, however, were freed from commercial considerations and now found fertile ground for their own visions, creating a completely new and fascinating style which has survived to the present day.

The Italian Neo-realist film school grew out of a desire to depict truth and reality after Mussolini's lies and deception, producing a series of highly dramatic films in an almost documentary style. The delightful posters for these films do not, however, have the power of the earlier posters by Hohenstein, Mataloni, Cappiello and the dramatic design for Gabriele D'Annunzio's *Cabiria* (1914) by Leopoldo Metlicovitz.

THE START

In the Poland of 1929 an avant-garde group of film theoreticians and enthusiasts, feeling that film had a more important role to play in society than the existing commercial fare, formed the START (Society of the Devotees of Artistic Film) association whose theories, though of little practical use at the time, had a great influence on the later development of Polish cinema. Aleksander Ford, a member of the group who had already made such films as *Lodz – the Polish Manchester* and *Awakening*, provided the link from this group through the horrors of the war into the

My Universities
Tadeusz Trepkowski
24¼ x 34/61.5 x 86
1948

Tadeusz Trepkowski began designing posters in 1931, using a great deal of symbolism and visual metaphors as evident here. In his poster for Mervyn Le Roy's *Random Harvest* of the same year, a huge key symbolizes Greer Garson's attempts to unlock Ronald Colman's memory, and his poster for Wanda Jakubowska's *The Last Stage* uses the simple device of a broken carnation against the striped material of a prison camp uniform.

Battle of the Rails
Henryk Tomaszewski
23½ x 34/60 x 86
1947

Tomaszewski began designing posters in 1936 and here employs the dynamic image of a speeding train for René Clement's first feature film.

post-war period. Under the new socialist state formed by the provisional government under Soviet supervision, Ford was appointed chief of the nationalized film organization, Film Polski, in 1945. The immediate post-war films dealt, not surprisingly, with the Nazi Occupation, the Ghetto and the Resistance. Wanda Jakubowska, another member of START, shocked filmgoers of 1948 with her film *The Last Stage* which depicted life in Auschwitz concentration camp, a fate she herself had endured.

Henryk Tomaszewski and Tadeusz Trepkowski, both born in 1914, were designing posters before the war, Trepkowski winning the Grand Prix at the 1937 Exposition Arts et Technique in Paris. His poster for *My Universities*, the third part of   *158* Mark Donskoy's 'Maxim Gorky' trilogy, was designed in 1948. The poster already deviates from the more sensational publicity assumed necessary by commercial organizations, specifically in the United States, by using the symbolism of the open book, walking stick and knapsack to suggest the nature of the film. Tomaszewski, a graduate of Warsaw Academy of Fine Arts, went on to receive the 1953 State Prize, the first prize at the 1953 Polish General Poster Exhibition and five prizes at poster exhibitions in Vienna, eventually becoming professor of the Warsaw Academy of Plastic Arts. His poster for *Black Narcissus* of 1948 shows a marked influence from   *163* the artist-designed posters produced for Ealing Studios in Britain. Another influence at this time is the work of A. M. Cassandre, whose bold mechanical shapes and dynamic realism have been emulated in Tomaszewski's *Battle of the Rails* and   *161* Biernacka and Wernerowa's *Brief Encounter* of 1947. Although *Brief Encounter* tells   *162* the story of a man and a woman meeting by chance on a railway station and falling in love, the poster artists have avoided any romantic imagery by using the red railway traffic signal to symbolize their brief encounter. Tomaszewski also designed the poster for Aleksander Ford's *Five from Barska Street* of 1953, an award-winning film   *172* which dealt with the rehabilitation of homeless delinquents.

Two of the world's leading film animators began their careers as poster designers in Poland. Walerian Borowczyk, who was born in 1923, studied at the Academy of Fine Arts in Cracow. He won the National Prize for his lithographic work in 1953 and began designing posters in 1954. *Le Jugement de Dieu* from 1955 hints   *168* at the macabre style developed in his later cartoons and live features. Jan Lenica, born in 1928, became assistant to Tomaszewski at the Academy in Warsaw and later collaborated with Borowczyk on many prize-winning cartoons. The two posters   *164* illustrated, *We Are All Murderers* (1952) and *Marriage in the Dusk*, present simple bold   *168* shapes, sometimes utilizing collage and cut-outs.

NEW SCHOOLS

With the death of Stalin in 1953 came a reaction against Socialist Realism. During the years before the establishment of Gomulka's anti-Stalinist government in 1956, Polish film-makers who had been dissatisfied with the state-run film industry founded the United Groups of Film Producers. Each group, or unit, consisted of sympathetic individuals who could set up their own style of production. For instance, Andrzej Wajda was a member of the highly respected KADR unit headed by Jerzy Kawalerowicz, director of *Under the Phrygian Star* which won an award at the 1955 Karlovy Vary Film Festival. With this new organization a new generation of film-makers evolved, turning frequently to the period of Nazi Occupation but with a fresh, psychological understanding. Andrzej Wajda's much acclaimed trilogy comprising *A Generation* (1955); *Kanal* (1957) and *Ashes and Diamonds* (1958) treated the years of occupation, uprising and liberation vividly, with a realism that presented the darker side of Polish romanticism. The poster for *Kanal*, reflecting the starkness of the film,   *176* was designed by Anczykowski who, unlike the majority of his fellow designers, used photographs for the basis of his designs.

Brief Encounter
Biernacka and
Wernerowa
23¼ x 34/59 x 86
1947

The tendency of Polish
film posters was to
summarize the film's
content in graphic terms.
In this case the artists
utilize a red railway signal
to symbolize the brief
encounter.

Black Narcissus
Henryk Tomaszewski
23¼ x 33/59 x 84
1948

The highly stylized
portrait in
Tomaszewski's poster is
of the provocative young
native girl, played by Jean
Simmons, in the Archers
production of *Black
Narcissus*.

We Are All Murderers
Jan Lenica
22¾ x 33½/58 x 85
1952

176	In 1959, Andrzej Munk, a former freedom fighter of the Polish underground, made the film *Bad Luck*, a satirical study of a man who tries hard to be a political conformist but is always out of step. The poster for this film, designed by Roman Cieslewicz, uses a collage of several hands to identify the hapless hero. This extremely busy design was succeeded the following year by his poster for Aleksander

166	Ford's *Knights of the Teutonic Order*, utilizing the powerful image of a fallen knight impaled to the ground by a colossal broadsword. The film was about the 14th-century battle of Grunwald, which had great national appeal.

Two brilliant artists who began designing posters in the early 1950s were Wiktor Gorka and Waldemar Swierzy. Gorka, a graduate from the Cracow School of Arts and Crafts, produced in 1952 an early poster for the Czech film *DS-70 is not Active*, which shows a keen understanding of colour and spacial relationships, a hallmark of all his

170	subsequent work. The poster for another Czech film, *Fearless*, was designed in 1957,

167	while the later *Cabaret* poster of 1973 is now considered a classic. Swierzy graduated from the Warsaw Academy and created the record of producing more posters than the prolific French designer Paul Colin, who died at the age of 94 with around 800 posters to his credit. Swierzy's preference for comedy is evident in the posters for

0,168	Fernandel's *The Law is the Law* (1958) and the East German *The Witches*. The red-

171	lipped *Midnight Cowboy* (1969) is another striking image from later years.

STAROWIEYSKI

Of all the poster artists who embodied the same creative spirit as the film-makers of the mid- to late 1950s, Franciszek Starowieyski stands alone. He captured all the angst, turmoil and suffering depicted in such films as *The Last Stage, Eroica, A Generation* and *Kanal* (1957), adding his own fantasies and transforming them all into some of the most bizarre images ever used in film poster design. Starowieyski was born in 1930 and studied at the Cracow School of Arts and Crafts. Practising painting, illustration, theatre design and graphics, he produced his first poster in 1956 for Mark Donskoy's *Mother*. In the same year he designed the poster for Grigori Chukhrai's

175	*The Forty First*, an internationally successful film of crucial importance to the renaissance of Soviet cinema. The film is a tragic love story of the Civil War, where a Red partisan falls in love with a White lieutenant. The primary image of the naked girl in Starowieyski's poster is taken directly from Edouard Manet's painting *Le Déjeuner sur l'herbe*, except that the girl is now holding a rifle instead of supporting her chin. To avoid an attack on her people she shoots the lieutenant with this rifle before he can return to his regiment.

181	Other early Starowieyski posters include the sombre, grey *La Loi des Rues* of

181	1956 and two humorous posters for *Stories Not From This Earth* and *The First Race*. In 1958 he designed the poster for the award-winning Hungarian film *House Under*

181	*the Rocks* directed by Karoly Makk. The overlapping imagery of the poster represents a scene from the film in which an ox-drawn cart confronts a wedding procession on

178	the same road. In the same year Starowieyski designed a poster for *Le Trois Font la Paire*, using a stylized image of a camera on a tripod, where the camera is a human eye and the eye is reflecting a murder. Also in 1958 he designed two highly surreal

174	posters: *St Peter's Umbrella*, depicting two winged devils praying beneath an

174	umbrella, and *Fanfare*, which represents a cow with a French horn as a head. Three

181	contrasting posters for 1960 are *Coloured Stockings*, an award-winning film about

182	children by Janusz Nasfeter; *Ninth Circle* and *Cossacks*.

Andrzej Wajda's early films analyze a highly traditional and proud people coming

179	to terms with an alien ideology. *Samson*, made in 1961, is the study of one such alien, a hunted Jew, escaping from the Ghetto during the Occupation. Starowieyski's poster of the collapsing wall symbolizes both Wajda's reworking of the Biblical story and the razing of the Warsaw Ghetto. The bold hand lettering and orange background

Knights of the Teutonic Order
Roman Cieslewicz
22¾ x 33½/58 x 85
¡960

Born in 1930, Roman Cieslewicz studied at the School of Arts and Crafts in his home town of Lvov from 1943 to 1945 and the Academy of Fine Arts in Crakow from 1949 to 1954. Originally influenced by Henryk Tomaszewski, his work revealed Expressionist tendencies (evident in *Knights of the Teutonic Order*) prior to his emigration to France in 1963. He has since been recognized as one of the world's foremost commercial artists.

Cabaret
Wiktor Gorka
22¾ x 33/58 x 84
1973

Winner of prizes at the National Film Poster Exhibition in Warsaw in 1956 and the International Film Poster Exhibition in Karlovy Vary in 1962, amongst many others, Wiktor Gorka's fluent designs have also been applied to the fields of public service, travel, sporting and circus posters, books and magazines.

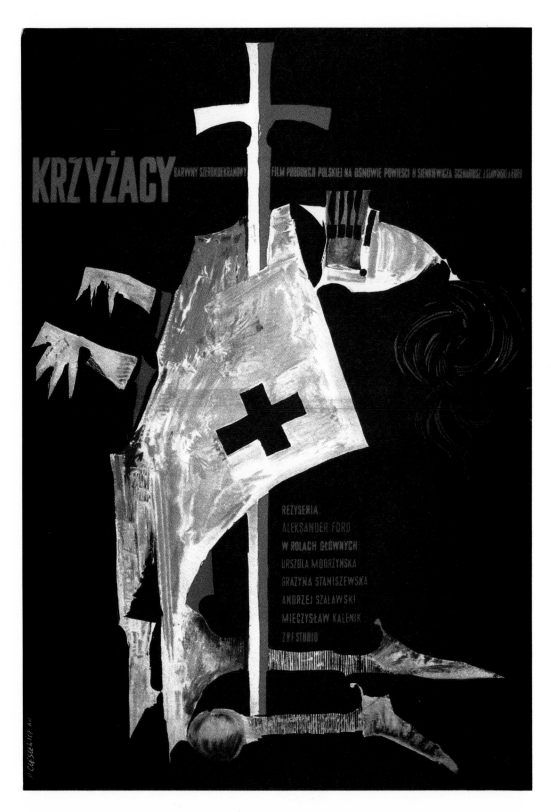

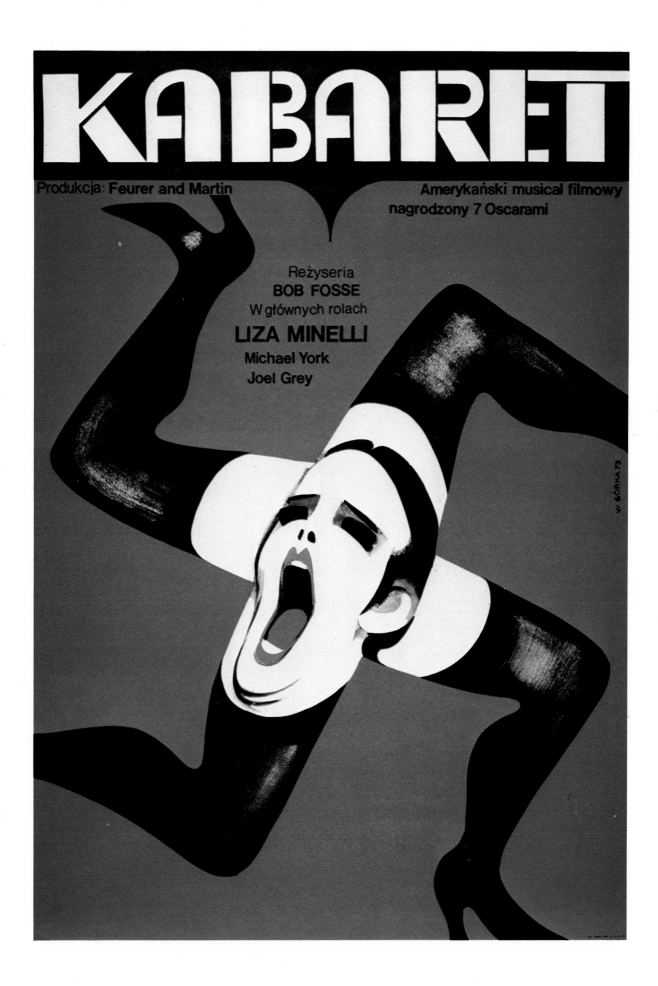

183 add to the visual power of this poster. *Everything For Sale* (1968) was Wajda's personal and introspective tribute to Zbigniew Cybulski, who had starred in three of his previous films and died tragically in 1967. In Starowieyski's poster, the almost liquid spectacles with the broken lenses are undoubtedly the dark glasses that Cybulski invariably wore. The hand lettering, in the same base colour as the artwork, blends in well with the overall design which now includes the artist's latest 'trade-mark', an unexplained series of circled numbers which, as in a child's puzzle, one feels tempted to join together.

In the 1970s Starowieyski surrendered himself entirely to the production of visual nightmares. Even the hand-written lettering takes on sinister qualities. Examples of
184 this work are the posters for Krzysztof Zanussi's *Illumination* (1973) and Wojciech
185 Marczewski's appropriate *Nightmares* (1978).

ITALIAN NEO-REALISM

On September 3rd 1943 Italy unconditionally surrendered to the Allies and with the fall of Mussolini, anti-Fascists from all walks of life were united in the struggle to liberate Italy from German Occupation. After the war, film-makers rejected all the old conventions and placed themselves at the service of their newly-liberated country to present life as it really was.

The scriptwriter Cesare Zavattini formulated the theory of cinematic Neo-realism, declaring that 'the artist's starting point must not be art but life itself . . .' and that the cinema '. . . must tell reality as if it were a story; there must be no gap between life and what is on the screen'. The public mood in the immediate post-war years was for escapism, however; people did not respond to the rather grim prospect of watching their own depressing reality.

The forerunner of Neo-realism, produced during the Fascist regime, was
187 Luchino Visconti's *Ossessione* (1942), the story of a casual labourer who becomes so infatuated with his employer that he willingly becomes her accomplice in the murder of her husband. The film was banned by Mussolini's government, whose policy was to keep crime and immorality from the screen in order to give the impression that Fascism was a cure for these human weaknesses. This powerful film, loosely based on James M. Cain's novel *The Postman Always Rings Twice* (1934) starkly displayed the internecine powers of violent sexual passion in a realistic working-class situation under Fascism, thus sowing the seeds of Neo-realism.

The first Neo-realist film to achieve international success was Roberto Rossellini's *Roma, Citta Aperta* (1945), depicting a war-torn Europe in a poignant, documentary style. A problem of Neo-realism was its inherent inability to depict absolute realism without some sort of groundwork, essential to the technique of telling a story in film. Even in *Roma, Citta Aperta*, certain scenes had to be shot in studio-built sets and the cast of non-actors so well rehearsed that, in a sense, they had become trained performers.

Vittorio De Sica also used non-actors in his classic Neo-realist film *Ladri di Biciclette* (1948). The story takes place in Rome, where an unemployed workman is offered a job as a bill sticker, as long as he owns a bicycle. He does, but has to pawn the family bed-linen to retrieve it. On his first day at work, he is pasting up a poster of Rita Hayworth when he sees the bicycle being stolen. Because of the constant theft of bicycles in Rome, his search for the thief and the stolen bicycle brings him up against constant official indifference. The workman finally traces the thief, who has now disposed of the bicycle, but as he tries to apprehend him the thief has an epileptic fit and the gathering crowd turns against him. Totally demoralized, he squats down on a curb with his son opposite a football stadium where, to make matters worse, the crowds swarm out of the gates mounted on bicycles. Subjected to more than he can stand, the workman hastily attempts to steal an unguarded bicycle but is immediately

Le Jugement du Dieu
Walerian Borowczyk
22¾ x 33½/58 x 85
1955

Walerian Borowczyk produced some unusual and bizarre poster images before embarking on a career as film animator and, eventually, feature film-maker.

The Witches
Waldemar Swierzy
23¼ x 33½/59 x 85

Marriage in the Dusk
Jan Lenica
22¾ x 34/58 x 86

Jan Lenica has been called the world's leading living posterist and is certainly revered by many of his contemporaries. His work on film posters brought him first prize at the International Film Poster Competition in 1962, one of many prizes awarded him in his part-time career as a poster designer.

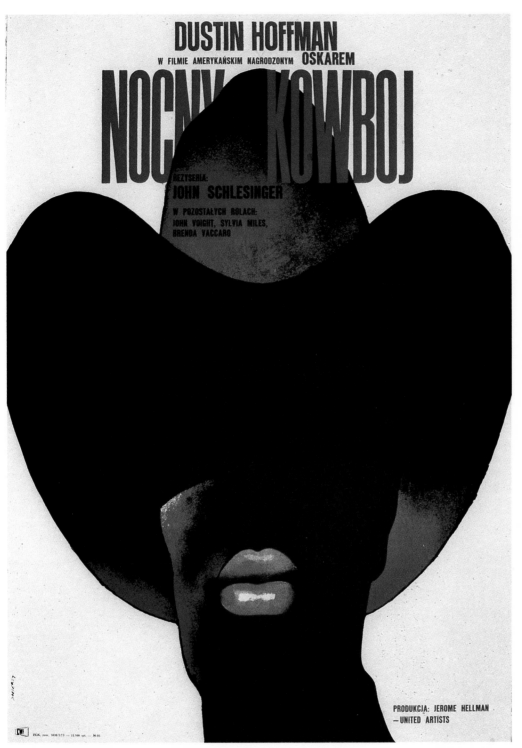

DUSTIN HOFFMAN
W FILMIE AMERYKAŃSKIM NAGRODZONYM OSKAREM
NOCNY KOWBOJ
REŻYSERIA:
JOHN SCHLESINGER
W POZOSTAŁYCH ROLACH:
JOHN VOIGHT, SYLVIA MILES,
BRENDA VACCARO

PRODUKCJA: JEROME HELLMAN
— UNITED ARTISTS

Fearless
Wiktor Gorka
22¾ x 33/58 x 84
1957

Midnight Cowboy
Waldemar Swierzy
22¾ x 32¼/58 x 82

Swierzy's desire for continually changing styles resulted in a move towards Pop Art in the mid-1960s, with posters such as *Midnight Cowboy*. His varying techniques were created in gouache, watercolour, crayon, pencil or acrylic, often in combination, and resulting in deceptively simple designs. However, he devotes around three weeks to each poster, producing five or six full-scale drafts before executing the final design. One of the most prolific of poster designers, his many prizes include the Award of the Central Cinema Board at the Film Poster Exhibition in Warsaw in 1956.

apprehended by the watchful owner. However, the look of total despair on the workman's face causes the understanding owner to drop the affair. The film ends with the workman's son, a witness to his father's demoralization, taking his hand to comfort him. Although the basic underlying problem of unemployment is not analyzed this does not detract from the film's vivid treatment of the disorganized post-war urban conditions.

186   The poster for *Ladri di Biciclette*, by E. Brini, is a bright impressionist composition of the film's protagonists, leaning more towards its warm-hearted aspects of father and son together, and the workman in a relaxed moment with his wife. A poster of stark realism at this time would not have attracted many filmgoers. Brini was not alone in disguising the depressing realism of these films with their more human features. The poster for Giuseppe de Santis' neo-realist *Riso Amaro* of 1949 dwells on the erotic content of the film; the wretched working conditions and labour of rice-growing are all but ignored.

191   Brini produced another poster in similar style for De Sica's *Miracolo a Milano*. Made in 1951, this film is also classed as Neo-realist, but has elements of fantasy reminiscent of René Clair. De Sica had to work as an actor to raise the money for *Miracolo a Milano*, which was scripted by Cesare Zavattini. Critical reaction was mixed but the elements of fantasy and working-class solidarity appealed to the public. In a poor, dilapidated village a young man's striving gains him the power to work miracles, which, at the end of the film, enables him to fly all the poor villagers to a better place. Once again Brini's poster depicts the allegorical side of the film and does not dwell on the plight of the villagers. Brini's style is therefore essentially non-realist.
188 Even his posters for Frank Capra's 'Why We Fight' documentaries, *The Battle of*
189 *Britain* and *Divide and Conquer*, both made in 1943, are symbolic in their reference to the topics described, the Battle of Britain being fought by two eagles, for instance.

        Even after the decline of the post-war realist style, claims were periodically made
185 for its revival. In 1960, for instance, Visconti's *Rocco e i Suoi Fratelli* was hailed as a return to Neo-realism, with its depiction of a poor southern family moving to Milan in order to better itself. The growing fraternal tension and the family's final hysterical destruction are presented, together with other events, in montage form on the poster. Non-actors were again used in 1964 in Pasolini's radically austere, near-
190 documentary version of *Il Vangelo Secondo Matteo*. But the anti-Fascist unity aroused by the 'War of Liberation' had been short-lived. The non-Marxist Neo-realist movement was considered to be too closely related to Communism in the ideas it reflected. Although finance for Italian production was already negligible, and American imports were having great success at the box office, the government appointed Giulio Andreotti to the department responsible for overseeing the performing arts. Controlled bank loans were restricted to the production of non-realist films, and films thought not to be in Italy's interest were banned. Such factors all added to Neo-realism's demise.

Five From Barska Street
Henryk Tomaszewski
22¾ x 33½/58 x 85
1953

Tomaszewski exploits a climactic scene from a publicity still to summarize the film.

Fanfare
Franciszek Starowieyski
23¼ x 33¼/59 x 84.5
1960

St Peter's Umbrella
Franciszek Starowieyski
22¾ x 33/58 x 84
1958

The Forty First
Franciszek Starowieyski
22¾ x 32½/58 x 82.5
1956

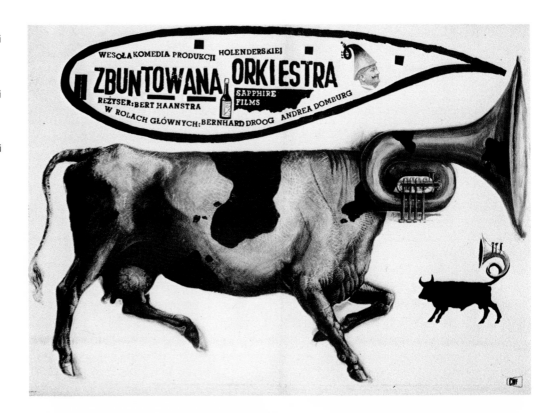

Kanal
Anczykowski
23¼ x 64¼/59 x 163
1957

An atypical Polish poster
employs a photocollage
of scenes from Andrzej
Wajda's tragic vision of
the Warsaw Rising,
August/September
1944.

Bad Luck
Roman Cieslewicz
22¾ x 32/58 x 81
1959

DS-70 is not Active
Wiktor Gorka
26¼ x 38½/67 x 98
1952

Le Trois Font la Paire
Franciszek Starowieyski
22¾ x 32¾/58 x 83
1958

Samson
Franciszek Starowieyski
22¾ x 33½/58 x 85
1961

The Law is the Law
Waldemar Swierzy
22¾ x 32¼/58 x 82
1958

Waldemar Swierzy's
early posters were full of
warmth and humour,
evident in *The Law is the
Law*.

Coloured Stockings
Franciszek Starowieyski
22¾ x 33½/58 x 85
1960

La Loi des Rues
Franciszek Starowieyski
22¾ x 32½/58 x 82.5
1956

**Stories Not From This
Earth**
Franciszek Starowieyski
22¾ x 33/58 x 84

**The House Under the
Rocks**
Franciszek Starowieyski
23 x 33/58.5 x 84
1959

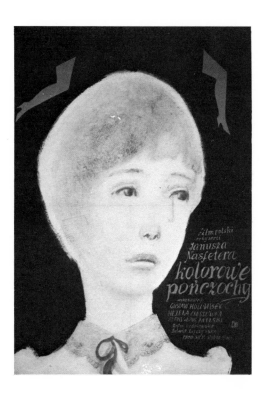

Ninth Circle
Franciszek Starowieyski
22¾ x 33½/58 x 85
1960

Everything For Sale
Franciszek Starowieyski
22¾ x 30½/57.5 x 77.5
1968

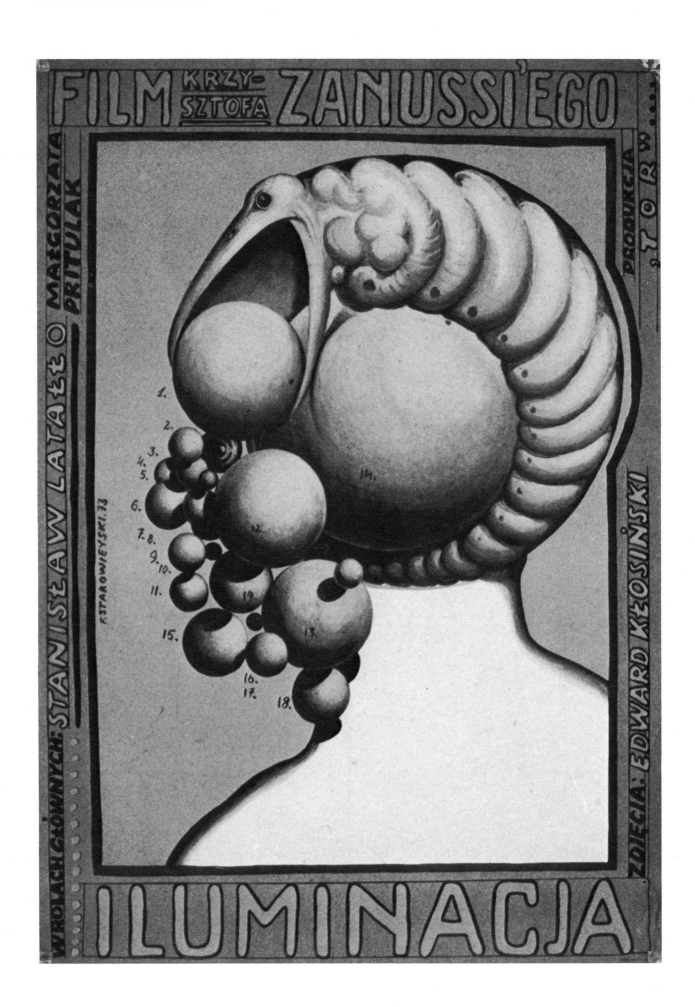

Illumination
Franciszek Starowieyski
22¾ x 30¼/57.5 x 77
1973

Nightmares
Franciszek Starowieyski
26¼ x 37¼/66.5 x 94.5
1978

Born in Cracow in 1930,
Franciszek Starowieyski
began designing posters
in 1956 and is now
considered one of the
world's leading
designers in this field. His
works have been
exhibited in Warsaw,
Paris, New York,
Philadelphia and
London, and his many
awards include the
Grand Prix at the
Exhibition of Film Posters
in Paris in 1975 and the
Grand Prix in Cannes the
same year. These
surrealistic designs,
executed in watercolour
and Indian ink and
completed in around two
weeks, are the results of
intensive study of each
film.

La Notte
40 x 56/101.6 x 142.2
1961

The poster represents
Marcello Mastroianni and
Jeanne Moreau in
Antonioni's film
describing the crisis in a
couple's crumbling
marriage.

Rocco e i Suoi Fratelli
40 x 56/101.6 x 142.2
1960

The poster portrays
events in montage for a
film which was hailed as
a return to Neo-realism.

Ladri di Biciclette
E. Brini
40 x 56/101.6 x 142.2
1948

Brini's colourful poster
reflects the warm-
hearted aspects of this
film, but belies its
uncompromising
treatment of post-war
unemployment.

Ossessione
40 x 56/101.6 x 142.2
1942

The poster for
Ossessione, Visconti's
first film and the
precursor of Neo-
realism, depicts Clara
Calamai as Giovanna
clinging to her lover Gino
(played by Massimo
Girotti) who is drawn into
conspiring in her
husband's murder.

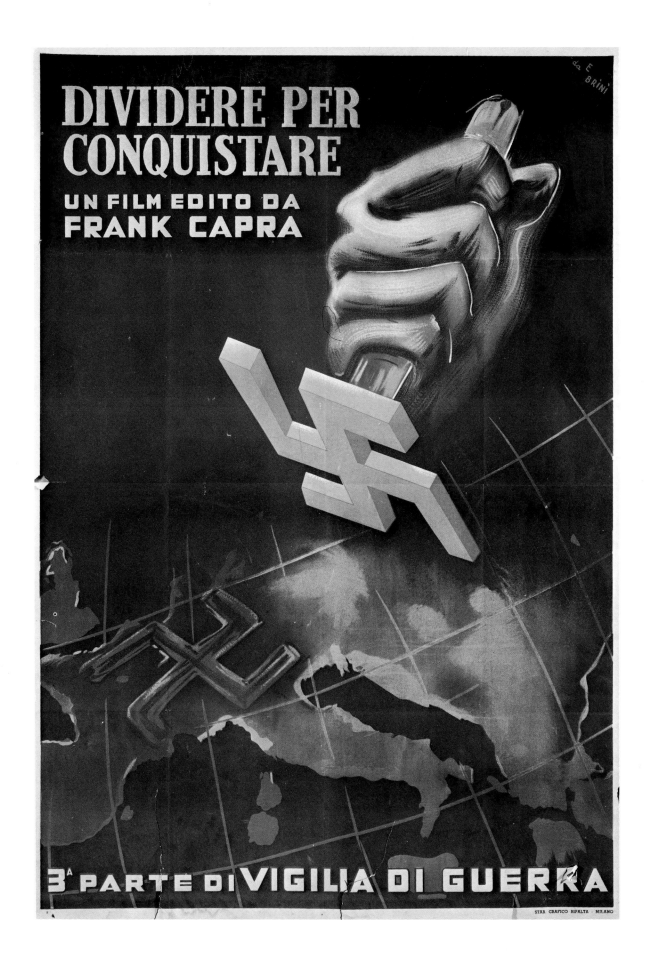

Divide and Conquer
E. Brini
40 x 56/101.6 x 142.2

The Battle of Britain
E. Brini
40 x 56/101.6 x 142.2

The lack of Neo-realist elements in post-war Italian film poster design is crowned by Brini's use of symbolism for Frank Capra's war documentaries.

Il Vangelo Secondo Matteo
40 x 56/101.6 x 142.2
1964

This dramatic image reflects Pasolini's ascetic, semi-documentary style.

Miracolo a Milano
E. Brini
56 x 80/142 x 203.2
1951

Once again Brini glosses over the squalid aspects of the film by portraying its more fantastical elements.

8 COMMITMENT AND ALIENATION
THE POWER OF THE IMAGE

Three months after the overthrow of the Batista regime in Cuba in 1959, the revolutionary government led by Fidel Castro, who proclaimed cinema as an art, set up the Cuban Institute of Cinematographic Art and Industry (ICAIC). This awareness of the validity of cinema as a tool in rebuilding society resulted in Cuba emerging in the 1960s as the most influential and progressive film-making country of the Third World. Third World cinema was, by implication, politically militant, with an international outlook evident in the documentaries of Julio Garcia Espinosa and Santiago Alvarez. Alvarez, who was head of newsreel production (Actualida des Cubanas), believed that art and politics were analogous and although early films were based on reform, such as *This Land of Ours* and *Housing*, Alvarez's *Hanoi, Martes 13*, made in 1967, was a powerful condemnation of America's role in the Vietnam War. Rostgaard's poster supports this indictment by turning bomb warheads into faces of President Lyndon B. Johnson.

The young artists emanating from ICAIC sought new ways to reflect revolutionary self-expression and anti-imperialism and, with official encouragement, produced a style which although based on national art forms, was aggressively contemporary. Although working in a Communist-based society, poster designers were given a great deal of freedom and borrowed various elements from Pop and psychedelic Art, comic-strips, American film and Polish theatre posters to add to their own national folk traditions.

Almost all the Cuban posters were created by silk screen process, a more economic technique than lithography in its use of space and machinery. Silk screen, in use from the 1920s, was developed from the stencil process that was known in China at the time of the Great Wall and the Egypt of the Pyramids. Then, the stencils were crude cut-outs in papyrus or fabric. The Japanese later sandwiched paper with silk thread to achieve more delicate designs and this laborious task subsequently

194

El Tigre Saltó y Mató Pero Morira . . . Morira . . .
Eduardo Bachs
13½ x 21½/34.3 x 54.6
1973

In the 1950s and 60s Third World Cinema dispelled the glossy myths propagated by Hollywood with the production of militantly political films. After the revolution in Cuba, the urgency of these films was transmitted by their compelling posters. Around 200 films were released in Cuba each year which, apart from domestic product, included other Third World films and some films from the West. Many Cuban artists submitted designs for each individual poster to the Cuban Institute of Cinematographic Art and Industry, thus creating work, and a wealth of stimulating graphic art.

Lucia
Raul Martinez
13½ x 21½/34.3 x 54.6
1968

Hanoi Martes 13
Alfredo Rostgaard
13½ x 21½/34.3 x 54.6
1967

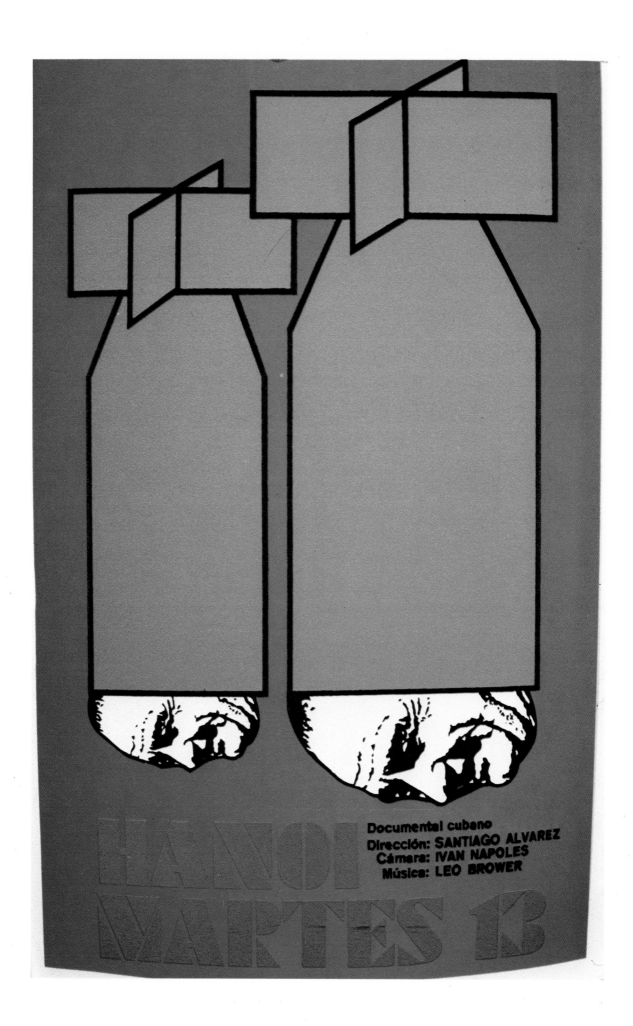

Documental cubano
Dirección: SANTIAGO ALVAREZ
Cámara: IVAN NAPOLES
Música: LEO BROWER

HANOI
MARTES 13

Caminos de Los Hombres
Luis Vega
13½ x 21½/34.3 x 54.6
1973

El Hombre de Maisinicú
Antonio Gonzalez
13½ x 21½/34.3 x 54.6
1973

Ukamau
Raymundo
13½ x 21½/34.3 x 54.6
1966

Sulkari
13½ x 21½/34.3 x 54.6

ended when the stencils were stuck directly onto woven silk. The next stage of stretching silk onto wooden frames resulted in the silk screen process.

The limitations of silk screen printing compared to lithography are in the degree of detail and tonal gradations obtainable. As with the Beggarstaffs' stencil printing, the Cuban posters look fresh and vibrant when compared to other posters of the period. Their high market value, resulting from the limited numbers printed, has been decried by the original designers, who saw the posters as useful items to be enjoyed and then thrown away. The posters were not in fact used to sell the films, as the cinemas were always packed to capacity anyway.

The first artists to emerge from ICAIC were Bachs, Rostgaard, Azcuy and Reboira. Bachs' posters include the bitingly satirical *El Tigre Saltó y Mató, Pero Morira . . . Morira . . .* (The Tiger Leaps and Kills, But it Will Die . . . Will Die . . .) of 1973. This was a short Cuban documentary, directed by Santiago Alvarez, about the Chilean folk singer Victor Jara who was killed by the ruling military junta. Two other posters by Bachs are *Por Primera Vez* (1968), a documentary by Octavio Ortazar, and *El Machete* (1975), directed by Juan Padron. *192*

Raul Martinez was a prominent Cuban painter who turned to graphics because he felt that painting dealt only with personal responses and problems posed by the artist himself, whereas the graphic artist must answer problems put to him by others. His designs drew elements from indigenous Cuban art forms which are evident in his poster for Humberto Solas' *Lucia* (1968), a study of women at three different stages in Cuban history. These forms are used as a base on which the more recent influences of psychedelic art are cast. *194*

Luis Vega used the comic strip for his poster of Richard Fleischer's *Blind Terror (Terror Ciego)* and Pop Art elements for his *Caminos de los Hombres*, both 1973. Raymundo also borrowed from Pop Art for his poster *Ukamau*. This was a Bolivian film directed by Jorge Sanjines, founder and director of the Bolivian National Film Institute, about the suffering of Indians. The film was considered 'too negative' by the government and Sanjines was promptly dismissed. Other posters to include elements of Pop Art were Antonio Gonzalez' *El Hombre de Maisinicú* (1973), a film by the Cuban director Manuel Perez and *Los Fusiles*, an explosive Brazilian film by Ruy Guerra. Julio Eloy's *Lo Viejo y lo Nuevo* was a 1977 reissue of Sergei Eisenstein's *The General Line*. *198 197 197 197 199 199*

The overall effect of Cuban posters on their society has been described by the Cuban writer and critic Edmundo Desnoes:

> 'In the houses, on the walls and windows, the new posters and billboards have replaced the painting of a flamingo, the North American calendar, magazines and advertisements for consumer goods and have introduced a new vision, a new preoccupation, without appealing to or exploiting sensationalism, sex or the illusion of aristocratic life.'

THE PHOTOGRAPHIC POSTER

A fundamental change in poster production occurred with the involvement of photographic techniques. A photographic negative is placed in firm contact with a plate coated in light-sensitive albumen solution and exposed to light. The hardened chemical coating is made insoluble to water and the area where light can pass through provides the image which will eventually be printed.

Unlike the silk screen process, photography has been an acceptable feature of poster design since the end of the First World War as a result of the work of photographers such as Arnold Genthe. In America, the photographic image became a regular ingredient of posters which were already naturalistic in representation, and by the late 1940s realistic, three-dimensional posters completely outweighed any abstract tendencies. This is particularly evident in the Warner Brothers' film posters.

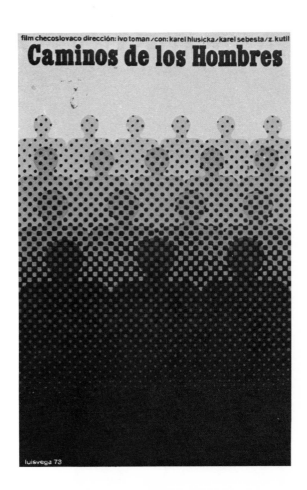

Terror Ciego
Luis Vega
13½ x 21½/34.3 x 54.6
1973

El Machete
Eduardo Bachs
13½ x 21½/34.3 x 54.6
1975

Los Fusiles
Antonio Gonzalez
13½ x 21½/34.3 x 54.6
1964

La Vendetta
13½ x 21½/34.3 x 54.6

Lo Viejo y Lo Nuevo
Julio Eloy
13½ x 21½/34.3 x 54.6
1977

Among the handful of designers who made exhaustive experiments with the new photographic techniques were El Lissitsky, Lazlo Moholy-Nagy, Man Ray, Jan Tschichold, Herbert Bayer and a few others. Moholy-Nagy, whose photograms first appeared in 1922, believed that photography was an integral feature of poster design.

> 'The new poster relies on photography, which is the new storytelling device of civilization, combined with the shock effect of new typefaces and brilliant colour effects, depending on the desired intensity of the message.'

In Germany during the late 1920s, the typographer Jan Tschichold put these ideas into effect with a series of film posters for the Phoebus Palast which combined photographs and sans-serif type in economical assymetrical compositions. A notable example is *Die Kameliendame (The Lady of the Camellias)* of 1927, starring Norma Talmadge. A green rectangle is imposed diagonally on a white ground and cut off at the right edge. In a red circle overlapping the top of the rectangle stands a photograph of the two stars. The lettering runs across the poster at right angles to the rectangle. As a contrast, in Japanese designs, the more elaborate typography employed is interwoven with photographs to produce more informal, but compelling results. The developing skills of photographic poster production in Japan resulted in the creation of some of the more outstanding film posters utilizing this process between the 1940s and early 1970s.

One of the earliest examples of the Japanese technique is for Akira Kurosawa's first feature *Sugata Sanshiro* (Judo Saga) of 1943. The poster consists of four *203* separate photographic images linked by the lettering which forms part of the overall design. This process is taken a stage further in Kurosawa's later *Ikimono No Kiroku* (Record of a Living Being), about the problems caused by the long-term effects of radiation. Here the poster's lettering is superimposed over the leading character's face, producing an almost three-dimensional effect. The Japanese designs always comprise several photographs, as in Naruse's *Ukigumo* (Floating Clouds) of 1955 and Kurosawa's *Yojimbo* (1961). *Yojimbo* tells the story of a lone Samurai who *204* wanders into a town ruled by two feuding families, each of which bids for his services as bodyguard ('yojimbo'). Obliging first one family and then the other, an incident causes him to deceive the more powerful employer and for this he is cruelly tortured. When the two gangs clash, the weaker side is mercilessly slaughtered, but during the carnage the Samurai manages to escape. Once recuperated, he returns in the role of professional soldier, challenging the entire surviving gang and wreaking vengeance in an explosive whirlwind finale. The poster represents Toshiro Mifune in action as the Samurai.

Technological developments have enabled designers to produce images in extremely fine detail, and in the 1970s German photolithographic posters equalled those of the Japanese. But whereas the Japanese still use photo-montage, most German posters employ one large, finely-detailed photograph, resulting in such exceptional images as Werner Herzog's *Aguirre der Zorn Gottes (Aguirre, Wrath of* *207* *God)*, of 1973 heralding the much-acclaimed new German cinema. The poster image depicts Klaus Kinski as Don Lope de Aguirre, a member of an expedition searching for El Dorado, whose usurpation of the company ends in hallucinations, the death of his daughter Flores (as seen in the poster) and final madness.

THE NEW GERMAN CINEMA

The seeds of the new German cinema lay in the Oberhausen manifesto of 1962, a document signed by a group of young film-makers led by the lawyer Alexander Kluge and resulting in the establishment of a Board of Curators of the Young German Film in 1965. This organization provided funds for first features including Kluge's own *Abschied Von Gestern* in 1966 and Werner Herzog's *Lebenszeichen* in 1968.

Herzog, unlike his contemporaries, studies people on the fringe of society and their metaphysical relationship with time and place, particularly the grotesque Aguirre in the tropical rain forests and Kasper Hauser in *Jeder Für Sich und Gott Gegen Alle (The Enigma of Kasper Hauser)* of 1975, who has been delivered into normal society after being kept in complete isolation for all his earlier life.

Contrariwise, the films of Rainer Werner Fassbinder deal with contemporary, and often controversial, human relationships. Fassbinder attended drama school and went on to found his own theatre in Munich with a group of regular collaborators. He became the most prolific of the new German film-makers, producing over thirty

208   features before his death in 1982. *Die Bitteren Tränen der Petra von Kant (The Bitter Tears of Petra von Kant)* of 1972 deals with a successful fashion designer who, after a short lesbian affair, experiences a series of distressing visits from her mother, her daughter and the other leading people in her life, who in the end desert her.

209   *Faustrecht der Freiheit (Fox)* of 1975 treats the subject of homosexuality with a notable lack of restraint. Fassbinder himself plays a young homosexual fairground worker who, after winning a lottery, is taken up by the 'smart set' only to be dropped by his new lover when the money runs out.

Wim Wenders' *Die Angst Tormanns Beim Elfmeter (The Goalkeeper's Fear of the Penalty)* of 1972 analyzes the protagonist's existential anxiety when, after spending the night with a cinema cashier, he strangles her and then wanders aimlessly through the German and Austrian border country so lost in himself that he makes no effort to evade capture. In 1974 this wandering is taken up again in *Alice in den Städten (Alice in the Cities)* when a German photographer returning from work in America helps the nine-year-old Alice, who has been deserted by her mother at the airport, to search the Ruhr valley for her grandmother's home with only a snapshot of the house as a clue. These two ideological tendencies of alienation and idealistic fellowship come together

205   in *Die Amerikanische Freund (The American Friend)*, produced by Wenders in 1977. Jonathan, a picture framer with a rare blood disease, is befriended by the mysterious Ripley and led into a series of nightmarish incidents of murder and Mafia revenge. The previous year Wenders directed the classic road movie *Im Lauf der Zeit (Kings of the Road)*, where Bruno and Robert meet on the road and travel together in Bruno's mobile workshop. Both men are lonely and alienated. Robert has left his wife and is totally dissatisfied with his former existence and Bruno travels aimlessly around repairing movie projectors. Their relationship is pushed to the limits and eventually they part.

The posters for all these films were produced by Filmverlag der Autoren, an organization set up by these and other young film directors in 1971 for the distribution and international sales of their films. The inherent simplicity of each poster helps to express the aesthetic originality of the new German cinema.

Por Primera Vez
Eduardo Bachs
13½ x 21½/34.3 x 54.6
1968

Yojimbo
20 x 28½/50.5 x 72.5
1961

The Japanese skills in
photolithography were
enhanced by their
sensitive fusion of
photocollage and
elegant typography,
resulting in many
evocative compositions.

東宝
黒沢明監督作品
椿三十郎
つばき さん じゅう
何を仕出かすか御存じ三十郎！
一閃宙に躍る逆抜き不意討ち斬り！
製作・田中友幸 菊島隆三
三船敏郎
仲代達矢
団令子
小林桂樹
九人の若侍
加山雄三
平田昭彦
太刀川寛
松井鍵三
田中邦衛
波里達彦
土屋嘉男
江原達怡
久保明
志村喬
藤原釜足
入江たか子
清水将夫
伊藤雄之助
東宝・黒沢プロ作品 東宝株式会社配給

Way of the Dragon
20¼ x 28½/51.4 x 72.4

Miyamoto Musashi
20¼ x 28½/51.4 x 72.4

Katsuben Dai Shashin
20¼ x 28½/51.4 x 72.4

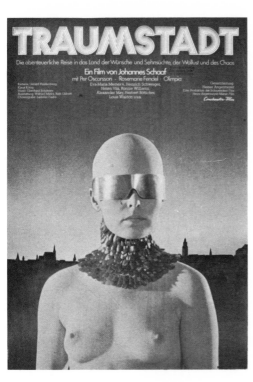

Alice in den Städten
23 x 32¾/58.5 x 83
1974

Im Lauf der Zeit
23 x 32¾/58.5 x 83
1976

Traumstadt
Sickert/Noss
23 x 33/58.4 x 83.8

Der Amerikanische Freund
23 x 32¾/58.5 x 83
1977

**Revenge of the
47 Samurai**
20¾ x 30½/52.6 x 77.4

Aguirre der Zorn Gottes
23 x 32¾/58.5 x 83
1973

The much-lauded new
German cinema of the
1970s was
complemented by
posters which, in
exploiting the new
techniques in
photolithography, were
capable of presenting
single large images in fine
detail.

Ein Film über die Leidenschaft schöner Frauen

Die bitteren Tränen der Petra von Kant

Ein Farbfilm von
R. W. Fassbinder

mit
Margit Carstensen
Hanna Schygulla
Irm Hermann
Katrin Schaake
Eva Mattes und
Gisela Fackelday
Kamera:
Michael Ballhaus

Prädikat: Besonders wertvoll

Rainer Werner Fassbinders faszinierendes Kammerspiel

FILMVERLAG
DER AUTOREN

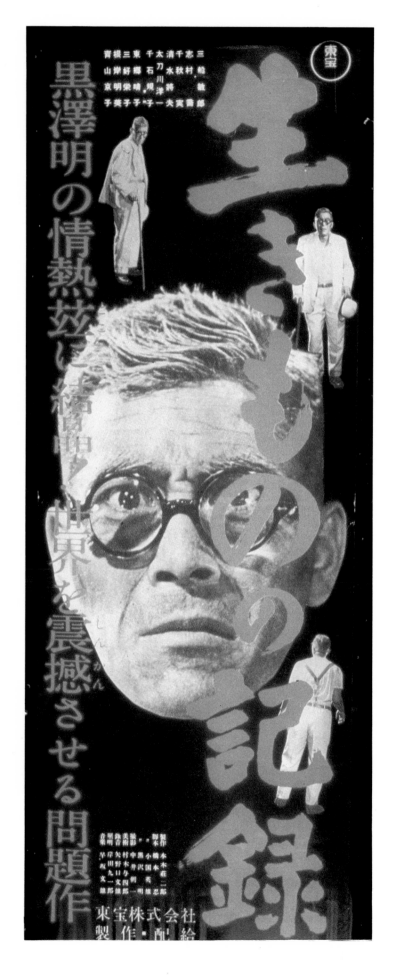

Ukigumo
1955

Ikimono No Kiroku
1955

Sugata Sanshiro
1943

9 NEW DIRECTIONS
DIVERSITY AND COLLECTABILITY

In the 1960s a profound dissatisfaction with modern values, particularly among the young, provoked a cynical reaction towards the establishment. This was reflected in a spate of extreme black comedies and the emergence of the underground film. Stanley Kubrick's *Dr. Strangelove, or How I Learned to Stop Worrying and Love the Bomb* (1964) was a black comedy on an imminent nuclear catastrophe precipitated by a deranged American general. The ensuing political burlesque was reiterated in cartoon form by Tomi Ungerer, whose posters already portrayed a 'sick' society.

Rebellion against this 'sick' society was engendered by the underground film, an alternative term for the avant-garde, which achieved a certain notoriety in New York with the films of Jack Smith, Kenneth Anger and Andy Warhol and their constant emphasis on sexuality. Andy Warhol's *The Chelsea Girls* (1966) was in fact the first underground film to attain commercial success. The three and a half hour-long film, utilizing the best of a series of half-hour takes at the Hotel Chelsea in New York, actually used seven hours of footage projected onto a split screen. Alan Aldridge's outlandish poster for the British release of *The Chelsea Girls* uses a style of eroticism disapproved by the establishment. The establishment's answer to these shock tactics was to borrow elements from the Pop Art movement, which in Britain emerged in 1956 with the opening of the exhibition 'This is Tomorrow' at the Whitechapel Art Gallery. Pop Art had grown from an interest in popular music, the comic strip and fashion, and these elements are evoked in various film posters including Harry Gordon's *Wonderwall* (1968), Ollé Frankzén's *The Trip* (1967) for Roger Corman and a reissue of Howard Hawks' *The Big Sleep* as well as the early work of Bob Peak such as *Modesty Blaise* (1966) and *In Like Flint* (1967). Peak's later posters include *The Missouri Breaks* (1976), *Excalibur* (1981), *Star Trek, the Motion Picture* (1979) and *Apocalypse Now* (1979). The last three posters are characterized by finely-detailed imagery and radiating light effects.

Dr. Strangelove
Tomi Ungerer
27 x 41/68.6 x 104.1
1964

The proximity of Tomi Ungerer's childhood home in Strasbourg to a wartime Nazi concentration camp provoked a morbid approach to his interest in drawing, which is now a hallmark of his work. Discovering Saul Steinberg in 1954 and becoming more involved in the American scene, he eventually went to the United States in 1956 and in a year was working for *Harper's* magazine, followed quickly by commissions from *Esquire, Life* and the *New York Times*, and was soon regarded as one of the top graphic artists in America.

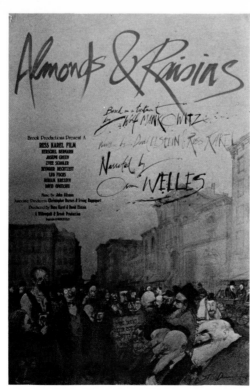

A Bigger Splash
David Hockney
30 x 40/76.2 x 101.6
1974

The poster image for
Jack Hazan's study of
David Hockney is taken
from the artist's *Portrait
of an Artist (Pool With
Two Figures).* The
painting was produced
in two versions. The first,
which was unsuccessful,
was started in 1971 and
the second in 1972, in
preparation for a New
York show.

Almonds and Raisins
Ralph Steadman
27 x 40/68.6 x 101.6

Ralph Steadman's
outrageous cartoons
have been popular for
some time. Like Gerald
Scarfe, his work is highly
appropriate to today's
cinema.

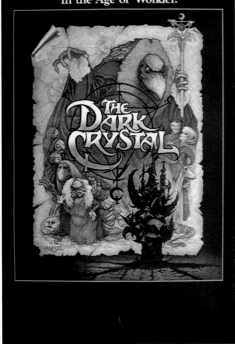

Lucky Lady
Richard Amsel
22 x 28/55.9 x 71.1
1975

The Dark Crystal
Richard Amsel
27 x 41/68.6 x 104.1
1982

Amsel's use of heavy
outline and ornamental
detail revives the Art
Nouveau style.

A major technical change in the 1960s was the introduction of new photographic techniques in printing, with the result that more and more posters utilized the photographic image. In Sweden this change was heightened in 1963 by a general reform which helped establish the Swedish Film Institute, bringing about a new generation of film-makers. The new poster imagery was then employed to reflect this reformation. Many of the film posters were designed by Bengt Serenander and incorporated a large photographic image, sometimes in close-ups bordering on the abstract, and a modicum of typography. Other trends in design include the revival of earlier styles, as in David Edward Byrd's *The Day of the Locust* (1975), with its Art *218* Deco motifs, and Richard Amsel's revitalized Art Nouveau style which exploits the device of the heavy outline in his posters for *Flash Gordon* (1980), *Nijinsky* (1980), *Murder on the Orient Express* (1974), *Julia, The Dark Crystal* (1982) and *Lucky Lady* *215* (1975).

Vic Fair produced fine posters for *Lisztomania* and *The Man Who Fell to Earth* (1976) and Frank Frazetta has continued his comic-book style illustration with posters for *After the Fox* (1966), *Yours, Mine and Ours* (1960) and *The Gauntlet* (1977). Posters by cartoonists now appear quite frequently, particularly *The Sunshine Boys* (1975) and *New York, New York* (1977) by Al Hirschfeld, *The Wall* (1983) by Gerald Scarfe and *Almonds and Raisins* by Ralph Steadman. Few artists have produced film *214* posters in recent years; *A Bigger Splash* (1974), which involved the work of David *214* Hockney, is a rare exception.

THE POSTER AS COLLECTIBLE

It is apparent from previous chapters that many artists *have* contributed to the production of film posters, and although art dealers in general have looked down on these works, owing to their predominantly unsigned and unnumbered multiple form, they are important artistically and historically, are visually stimulating and, to some degree, depending on age, available.

In general, film posters are cheaper to buy than other forms of graphic design by known artists and may be of equal, if not greater, importance than original work. Anyone attempting to collect original art nowadays would in any case require huge resources. Film posters by the likes of Norman Rockwell, Ronald Searle, Bernard Lancy or even Jules Chéret, on the other hand, are still accessible to anyone of modest means and, from their very nature of being posted up and then thrown away, are in themselves rarities. The interest of collecting film posters is in sometimes not knowing what the poster for a particular film is like. One can, of course, be disappointed, but this seems to be always outweighed by eventually finding a great poster for a great film.

Other reasons for collecting film posters are varied and arbitrary. For many collectors it gives pure enjoyment and complements their individual interests in the cinema. Collecting by star is by far the most common practice, although this varies from the enthusiast who pins posters to the wall with abandon until they are eventually torn down, to the meticulous hoarder whose posters are carefully preserved in filing cabinets with lists always at hand. The same applies to the genre collector, of whom the best known is probably Forrest J. Ackerman, editor of *Famous Monsters of Filmland*, whose 'Ackermansion' in Hollywood is bursting with ephemera and literature relating to science-fiction. This type of collector has been dubbed 'FOOF' in America, for Fans of Old Film. One of the major all-round FOOFs is Jane Withers, who began collecting film ephemera as a child star in the 1930s. Her collection has not only taken over her home but moved into several warehouses as well. Of course, FOOFs do not limit themselves solely to film posters; they also collect anything relating to their field — autographs, magazines, stills, props and so on. The collector of cinema posters *per se* is a member of a much smaller circle.

THE COST OF COLLECTING

Film poster collecting is in its infancy, as can be gauged by comparative prices for the following American posters taken from various catalogues and auctions over the last twenty years. All prices given are in American dollars.

The Passage to Marseilles 1944 Humphrey Bogart
Prices for a 27" x 41" 1-sheet
1965 $8.50
1976 $50
1984 $300
The Bank Dick 1940 W. C. Fields
1965 $15 for a 1-sheet
1982 $525 for a 14" x 36" insert card
Birth of a Nation 1915 D. W. Griffith
1965 $20 for an 11" x 14" lobby card
1970 $300 for a 1-sheet
1977 $5000 for a 1-sheet
The Magnificent Ambersons 1942 Orson Welles
Prices for a 1-sheet designed by Norman Rockwell
1965 $15
1978 $450
Gentlemen Prefer Blondes 1953 Marilyn Monroe
Prices for a 1-sheet
1965 $10
1976 $50
1981 $100
Jailhouse Rock 1957 Elvis Presley
Prices for an insert card
1976 $15
1977 $45
1982 $125

In 1965 a collector could acquire 1-sheets for *Destry Rides Again*, the 1939 version of *The Hound of the Baskervilles* and *Idiot's Delight* with Norma Shearer for $15 each. A 1-sheet for *The Wizard of Oz* would have cost $12 and 50 cents and a 1-sheet for *Mildred Pierce* $7 and 50 cents! Things started moving in 1977 when a 3-sheet for *The Maltese Falcon* sold for $900, a 1-sheet for *Citizen Kane* was sold at $1100 and the German *Hamlet* reached $1250. A 1-sheet for *Casablanca* reached the same price the following year and in 1981 a 3-sheet for *City Lights* and a German poster for *Grand Hotel* were both sold at $3000 each.

Some posters have become valuable as a result of rapid campaign changes, title changes or censor demands. For example, the first British *Star Wars* poster was designed by the Hildebrandts, but by the time the film was on general release the posters had been changed to a new design by Chantrell. That first poster now carries a price tag of around £100. George Lucas continued to tease the market with the title change of *Revenge of the Jedi* to *Return of the Jedi*. American prices on *Revenge* are already around $40.

To the serious researcher, film poster collecting can be very frustrating. Can one actually accomplish anything and make some sort of contribution to this field? Any long-standing value will depend on the artistic, cultural and historical character of the collection. Film institutes have been collecting posters for some time, but as this pursuit is as yet in its infancy there is still great satisfaction to be gained from participating in the rescue and preservation of these crucial works.

The Missouri Breaks
Bob Peak
27 x 41/68.6 x 104.1
1976

An extremely versatile
film poster designer, Bob
Peak's highly individual
and developing style has
been augmented by a
flair for fine and accurate
detail.

The Day of the Locust
David Edward Byrd
27 x 41/68.6 x 104.1
1975

A leading American
theatrical poster
designer, David Edward
Byrd gained prominence
in the early 1970s with
his posters for the
musicals *Godspell,
Jesus Christ Superstar*
and *Follies*. His style is
tinged by Art Deco and in
fact he produced a
poster for the first New
York Art Deco Exposition
at the Radio City Music
Hall in 1974.

**The Man Who Fell to
Earth**
Vic Fair
27 x 40/68.6 x 101.6
1976

A fine composition,
noted by its popularity
amongst collectors, to
promote Nicolas Roeg's
ambitious science fiction
parable.

Bibliography

Ackerman, Forrest J. *Souvenir Book of Mr. Science Fiction's Fantasy Museum.* Japan: Tsurumoto Room, 1978.

Ades, Dawn. *The 20th-Century Poster. Design of the Avant-Garde.* New York: Abbeville Press, 1984.

Amstutz, Walter. Ed. *Who's Who in Graphic Art.* Zurich: The Graphis Press, 1962.

Balázs, Béla. *Theory of the Film.* New York: Dover, 1970.

Barnicoat, John. *A Concise History of Posters.* London: Thames & Hudson, 1979.

Barnouw, Erik. *Documentary.* London, Oxford, New York: Oxford University Press,1974.

Barr, Charles. *Ealing Studios.* London: Cameron & Tayleur, 1977.

Bojko, Szymon. *The Polish Poster Today.* Warsaw: Author's Agency, 1972.

Borga, J.-M. & Martinand, B. *Affiches du Cinema Français.* Paris: Editions Delville,1977.

Capitaine, Jean-Louis & Charton, Balthazar J. M. *L'Affiche de Cinema.* Paris: Editions Frederic Birr. Atelier Henry Labat, 1983.

Clarens, Carlos. *Horror Movies.* London: Panther, 1971.

Constantine, Mildred & Fern, Alan. *Revolutionary Soviet Film Posters.* Baltimore & London: Johns Hopkins, 1974.

Durgnat, Raymond. *Durgnat on Film.* London: Faber & Faber, 1976.

Eckersley, Tom. *Poster Design.* London & New York: Studio Publications, 1954.

Eisenstein, Sergei. *The Film Sense.* London: Faber & Faber, 1955.

Elliott, Brian. *Silk-Screen Printing.* London: Oxford University Press, 1971.

Fishendon, R. B. Ed. *The Penrose Annual.* London: Lund Humphries, 1949.

Fuksiewicz, Jacek. *Polish Cinema.* Warsaw: Interpress, 1973.

George, Waldemar. *Expressionism.* London: Thames & Hudson, 1960.

Gilmour, Pat. *Artists at Curwen.* London: The Tate Gallery, 1977.

Halliwell, Leslie. *Halliwell's Filmgoer's Companion.* London: Paladin, 1979.

Hammond, Paul. *Marvellous Méliès.* London & Bedford: Gordon Fraser, 1974.

Katz, Ephraim. *The International Film Encyclopedia.* London: Papermac, 1982.

Kracauer, Siegfried. *From Caligari to Hitler.* New York: Princeton Unversity Press,1966.

Leyda, Jay. *Kino.* London: George Allen & Unwin, 1983.

Manvell, Dr. Roger. Ed. *The International Encyclopedia of Film.* London: Rainbird Reference Books, 1972.

Manvell, Roger & Heinrich Fraenkel: *The German Cinema.* London: J. M. Dent & Sons,1971.

Michatek, Boleslaw. *The Cinema of Andrzej Wajda.* London: Tantivy, 1973.

Moholy-Nagy, Lazlo. *The New Typography.* New York: Praeger, 1970.

Morgan, Ann Lee. Ed. *Contemporary Designers.* London: Macmillan, 1984.

Murray, Peter & Linda. *A Dictionary of Art and Artists.* Harmondsworth: Penguin,1966.

Muller-Brockman, Josef and Shizuko. *History of the Poster.* Zurich: ABC Verlag,1971.

Nemeskürty, István. *Word and Image.* Hungary: Corvina, 1974.

Nicholls, Bill. Ed. *Movies and Methods.* Berkeley, Los Angeles, London: University of California Press, 1976.

Perry, George. *Forever Ealing.* London: Pavilion, 1981.

Pevsner, Nikolaus. *Pioneers of Modern Design.* Harmondsworth: Penguin, 1966.

Renan, Sheldon. *An Introduction to the American Underground Film.* New York: Dutton, 1967.

Rennert, Jack. *100 Years of Circus Posters*. New York: Avon Books, 1974.

Renoir, Jean. *My Life and My Films*. London: Collins, 1974.

Reynolds, Charles and Regina. *100 Years of Magic Posters*. New York: Darien House, 1976.

Rice, Tamara Talbot. *A Concise History of Russian Art*. London: Thames & Hudson, 1963.

Sadoul, Georges. *French Film*. London: Falcon Press, 1953.

Schapiro, Steve & David Chierichetti. *The Movie Poster Book*. New York: E. P. Dutton, 1979.

Sprigge, Elizabeth & Kihm, Jean-Jacques. *Jean Cocteau: The Man and the Mirror*. London: Victor Gollancz, 1968.

Steinberg, S. H. *Five Hundred Years of Printing*. Harmondsworth: Penguin, 1966.

Terry, Walter & Rennert, Jack. *100 Years of Dance Posters*. New York: Darien House, 1975.

Thomson, David. *A Biographical Dictionary of the Cinema*. London: Secker & Warburg, 1975.

Tyler, Parker. *Classics of the Foreign Film*. London: Spring Books, 1966.

Vorontsov, Yuri & Igor Rachuk. *The Phenomenon of the Soviet Film*. Moscow: Progress, 1980.

Williams, Christopher. Ed. *Realism and the Cinema*. London: Routledge & Kegan Paul, 1980.

Williams, Robert C. *Artists in Revolution*. London: Scolar Press, 1978.

Wilson, David. Ed. *Projecting Britain*. London: BFI, 1982.

Wollen, Peter. *Signs and Meaning in the Cinema*. London: Thames & Hudson, Cinema One, 1970.

Collections

Masters of the Poster. London: Academy Editions, 1978.

Soviet Cinema Poster, The. Leningrad: Aurora Art, 1983.

Catalogues

Affiches Françaises du Cinema Muet. Lyon-Monplaisir: Institut Lumière. Exhibition catalogue.

Edward Ardizzone. A retrospective exhibition. London: Victoria and Albert Museum. 1973–74.

John Minton 1917–57. An exhibition of painting and drawings. 1979.

Poster Pleasures. New York: Phillips, 1981. Auction catalogue.

Svenska Filmaffischer. Nationalmuseum Svenska Filminstitutet. Risbergs Tryckeri AB, Uddevalla, 1983. Exhibition catalogue.

Tate Gallery, an Illustrated Companion, The. London: Tate Gallery, 1979.

Tom Eckersley: Posters and other graphic works. London: A Camden Arts Centre exhibition, 1980.

Tomi Ungerer Exhibition. Koln: Argos Press, 1981.

Periodicals

Art and Industry. 1949.

Focus on Film. The Tantivy Press. No. 20, Spring, 1975.

Graphis. The Graphis Press. Zurich. 1948.

In Cinema. In Cinema Ltd., New York. June 1981, Volume 1 Issue 8.

Life. Time Inc., Chicago. October 1981, Volume 4 Number 10.

Movie, The. London: Orbis, 1980–1982.

Print. New York. 1965.

Studio International. London. 1973.

Index

A. B. See Lithograph Company
54, 55
Abschied von Gestern 201
Ackerman, Forrest J. 216
Aguirre, der Zorn Gottes 200, 207
Aldridge, Alan
The Chelsea Girls 213
Alice in den Städten 201, *205*
Allard, Georges
Les Enfants du Paradis 141,
151
Allen and Sons, David 13, 14
Alvarez, Santiago 192, 193, 196
American Entertainment
Company 14
American Vitagraph Incorporated
55, 56, 58, 59
Amerikanische Freund, Die 201,
205
Amsel, Richard
The Dark Crystal 215, 216
Flash Gordon 216
Julia 216
Lucky Lady 215, 216
Murder on the Orient Express
216
Nijinsky 216
Anczykowski
Kanal 160, 165, *176*
Anna Christie 68, *82*
Archipenko, Alexander 39
Ardizzone, Edward 111
The Magnet 121
Nicholas Nickleby 111, *121*
Art Deco 30, 31, 36, 45, 65, 133,
137, 143, 144, 216
Art Nouveau 10, 23, 39, 215, 216
Associated British Pathé 111, 128
Auzolle
Cinématographe Lumière 14,
20
Azcuy 196

Bachs, Eduardo 196
El Machete 196, *199*
*El Tigré Saltó y Mato Pero
Morira . . . Morira . . .* 192,
193, 196
Por Primera Vez 196, *202*
Balcon, Michael 105, 108, 118
Band Wagon 68, *81*
Bank Dick, The 217
Barkleys of Broadway, The 68, *80*
Barrère, Adrien
Tous y menent leurs enfants!
15, *20*
Bass, Saul 73
Advise and Consent 73
Anatomy of a Murder 73, *99*
Bonjour Tristesse 73
The Cardinal 73
Carmen Jones 73
Death of a Salesman 73
Exodus 73, *102*
Love in the Afternoon 73
Man with the Golden Arm 73,
98, 99
No Way Out 73, *103*
North by Northwest 73
One, Two, Three 73, *102*
Psycho 73
Saint Joan 73, *101*
Vertigo 73, *100*
Baubelski, Adam 159
Bawden, Edward 114, 117
Hue and Cry 108, *109*, 116
The Titfield Thunderbolt 111,
114
Bayer, Herbert 200
Beardsley, Aubrey 11, 61, 65
Beckman, Max 23
Beddington, Jack 122
Beggarstaffs, The 11, 111, 127,
196

Belinsky, Constantin 145
Benoit-Levy, J. 145
Bentley, Nicolas 108
Benton, Thomas Hart
The Grapes of Wrath 72
Berlin Die Sinfonie der Grosstadt
22, 23, 33
Berry, William Edward 112, 113
Bertrand, Jean
La Nuit du Carrefour 137, *142*,
143
Bête Humaine, La 137, *140*, 141
Biernacka and Wernerowa
Brief Encounter 160, 162, *163*
Big Parade, The 60
Bilinsky, Boris
Mauprat 133
Biophonographe, Le 15, *19*
Biro, Mihaly 17
Birth of a Nation, The 63, 76
*Bitteren Tränen der Petra von
Kant, Die* 201, *208*, 209
Black man 112
Black Pirate, The 64, *69*
Blaue Reiter, Der 23
Blue Angel, The 72
Blue Skies 68, *83*
Boccioni, Umberto 39
Bogart, Humphrey 68, 85, 86
Bograd, Iosif 40
Bojko, Szymon 45
Bolwieser 209
Bonneaud, Jacques
Les Enfants du Paradis 141,
151
Borisov, Grigory and Pyotr
Zhukov
The Living Corpse 47, 49
Borowczyk, Walerian
Le Jugement du Dieu 160, *168*
Boswell, James
The Blue Lamp 111, *122*
The Brave Don't Cry 111, 116,
128
It Always Rains on Sunday 111,
122
The Pool of London 111, *114*
Bourgeois, Djo
L'Inhumaine 133, *138*, 139
Bow, Clara 72, 95
Bradley, Will 10, 11
Bratby, John 113, 128
Bresson, Robert 144, 155
Bride 13 64, *75*
Brighton Rock 111, *127*
Brini, E.
The Battle of Britain 173, *189*
Divide and Conquer 173, *188*,
189
Ladri di Biciclette 173, *186*
Miracolo a Milano 173, 190,*191*
Brispot, Henri
Cinématographe Lumière 14
Brisset 10
Brooks, Louise 30, 31, 33, 36
Brown, Clarence 65, 74, 78, 82
Browne, Tom 14
Brücke, Die 30
Bucher-Crosmières, Huguette
145
Büchse der Pandora, Die 31, 33,
36
Butts Lithograph Company 64
Byrd, David Edward
The Day of the Locust 216, *218*
Bysouth, Brian 112

Cabiria 132, 159
Cagney, James 68, 85, 86, 92,
102
Camille 61
Cappiello, Leonetto 132, 159
Judex 132
Capra, Frank 173, 188, 189
Carlu, Jean 145
Carné, Marcel 141, 144, 148,
150, 151
Cartier, Roger 145
Casablanca 68, *87*, 217
Cassandre, A. M. 160
Castro, Fidel 193
Cavalcanti, Alberto 111, 133
Caxton, William 9
Cerutti, Henri 137
L'Atalante 137
Chaix, Albert 13
Chaney, Lon 65, 76
Chantrell
Star Wars 217

Chaplin, Charles 56, 59, 76
Chapman, George
The Ghost of St Michaels 105
Charity Bazaar Fire, The 15
Cheat, The 132
Chéret Jules 10, 13, 14, 132, 216
Pantomimes Lumineuses 12,
13, 14
Projections Artistiques 15
Cieslewicz, Roman 166
Bad Luck 165, *176*
Knights of the Teutonic Order
165, *166*
Cinématographe Perfectionné
15, 20, *21*
Citizen Kane 65, *77*, 217
City Lights 217
City Symphonies 33, 44
Clair, René 133, 139, 141
Cocteau, Jean 144, 154, 155
Le Testament d'Orphée 144,
156, *157*
Colbert, Claudette 68, 82
Colin, Jean 144, 153
Sortilèges 144, *152*, 153
Zero de Conduite 144
Colin, Paul 155, 165
*Un condamné a mort s'est
echappé* 144
*Journal d'un curé de
campagne* 144, *155*
Colour men 112
Colour offset lithography 65, 112
Columbia Pictures 64, 89
Constructivism 33, 39, 41, 42,
44, 51
Cooper, Gary 72, 94, 95
Coulet, Louis
Salle de l'Etoile 15, *16*, 17
Courtenay, Tom 129
Cousins, Les 144
Crichton, Charles 108, *109*
Crosby, Bing 82, 83
Crowd, The 60
Cry, The 23
Cuban Institute of
Cinematographic Art, The
193, 202
Cubism 39, 44, 47, 139, 144
Cucaracha, La 68, *78*, 79
Cuny, Alain 133
Feu Mathias Pascal 133
Curwen Press, The 117
Cybulski, Zbigniew 169

Dada 40, 42
Danischewsky, Monja 105, 111
Daumier, Honoré 10
De Mille, Cecil B. 55, 60, 66, 67,
132
De Sica, Vittorio 169, 173, 186,
191
Déjeuner sur l'herbe, Le 165
Delluc, Louis 132
Dempster, Carol 64
Derouet, Edgard 137
Desnoes, Edmundo 196
Destiny 30
Destry Rides Again 217
Diary of a Lost Girl 33
Dietrich, Marlene 72, 89, 94, 95
Direct lithography 112, 116
Dlugach, Mikhail 40
Don Q, Son of Zorro 64, *71*
Donaldson Show Print Company
15
Donskoy, Mark 160, 165
Dovzhenko, Alexander 50, 51
Dream Street 64, *70*
Dreville, Jean 149
Dubout, Albert
César 137, *147*
Fanny 137, *147*
Marius 137, *146*
Duccio-Marvasi
Napoléon 133, *140*
Duck Soup 65, *75*

Eagle, The 64, *70*, 76
Ealing Studios 105, 108–109,
110–111, 113, 114–125, 160
Eckersley, Tom 118
Whisky Galore! 108, 118, *119*
Eckman, Gosta 27
Edison, Thomas 14, 55, 56
Eggeling, Viking 30, 33
Eisenstein, Sergei 40–42, 44, 49,
52, 196
Elfer, Arpad 128

Eloy, Julio
Lo Viejo y lo Nuevo 196, *199*
Elusive Pimpernel, The 111, *127*
*Enough Simplicity in Every Wise
Man* 42
Epstein, Jean 133
Erdgeist 36
Ermler, Friedrich 42, 43, 45
Eroica 165
Etaix, Pierre 144
Mon Oncle 144, *153*
Expressionism 23, 24, 26, 28, 30,
33, 36, 39, 166

Fair, Vic
Lisztomania 216
The Man Who Fell to Earth 216,
218, *219*
Fairbanks, Douglas 46, 47, 49,
64, 69, 71
Faria, Candido Aragonese de 15,
132, 141
A la conquète du Pôle 130, 131
Farrar, Geraldine 60, 66, 67
Fassbinder, Rainer Werner 201
Faust 31
Faustrecht der Freiheit 201, *209*
Felix, Maria 132
Fenneker, Josef 27
Carmen 27
Der Januskopf 27
Fernandel 137, 143, 165, 180
Ferraci, René 156
Elena et les hommes 156
La Mariée était en noir 145, *156*
Feuillade, Louis 15, 132, 141
Feyder, Jacques 133, 141
Fields, W. C. 217
Fight in the Thieves' Kitchen 106,
107
Film Polski 160
Filmverlag der Autoren 201
Finney, Albert 129
Fires Were Started 108
Fitton, James 108
Kind Hearts and Coronets 108,
114, *115*
Meet Mr Lucifer 111
Flemeng, François 15
Flesh and the Devil 65, *78*
Flynn, Errol 68, 84
Foldes, Imres 17
Folon, Jean-Michel 149
FOOFs 216
For Heaven's Sake 64, *71*
For Them That Trespass 111, *128*
Forbidden Planet 73, *96*
Ford, Aleksandr 159, 160, 165
Fourasie, J. 141, 151
François, Fernand 149
Frankenstein 28
Frankzen, Olle
The Big Sleep 213
The Trip 213
Fraser, Eric 108, 117
Fratini, Renatto 112
Frazetta, Frank
After the Fox 216
The Gauntlet 216
Yours, Mine and Ours 216
Freedman, Barnett 108, 117
Johnny Frenchman 117
Freund, Karl 33
Friedlander, Adolf 13
Friedlander, Adolf 13
Futurism 39, 44, 47

Gabin, Jean 137, 139, 140
Gabo, Naum 40
Gance, Abel 133, 137
Garbo, Greta 65, 78, 82, 217
Gaumont, Leon 15, 132, 133
General Film 55, 56
Generation, A 160, 165
Genie du Mal, Le 58, 59
Genthe, Arnold 196
Gentlemen Prefer Blondes 217
Gerard, Michel 149
Gerasimovich, Iosif 40
The New Babylon 48, 49·
Géricault, Théodore 9
Ghost-of Slumber Mountain, The
64, *67*
Gid, Raymond 149
Gilbert, John 65, 78
Girl from Missouri, The 72, *90*
Giscard, Henry 149
Gish, Lillian 60
Glasgow School of Art 10
Gold and Glitter 54, 55, 56

Golem, Der 26, *28*
Goncharova, Natalia 39
Gonzalez, Antonio
    El Hombre de Maisincu 196, *197*
    Los Fusiles 196, *199*
Gordon, Harry
    Wonderwall 213
Gorka, Wiktor 166
    Cabaret 165, 166, *167*
    Ds-70 is not Active 176, *177*
    Fearless 165, *170*, 171
Gorky, Maxim 17, 137
Goskino 40
Goya, Francisco 9
Grable, Betty 72, 89
Grand Hotel 217
Grande, G. 15
Granger, Stewart 111
Great Lie, The 68
Greenwood, Joan 108, 111
Greiffenhagen, Maurice
    Pall Mall Budget 11
Grierson, John 125
Griffith, D. W. 54–56, 60, 62–64, 70, 76
Grinsson, Boris 149
Gris, Juan 39
Gronowski, Tadeusz 159
Grosz, Georg 40, 42
Group 3 111, 118
Guazzoni, Enrico 56, 64
Guerra, Ruy 196
Guillaume, Albert 149
Guinness, Alec 110, 111, 118

Hamilton, Richard 213
Hamlet (1920) 27, 30, *31*
Hamlet (1942) 108, 113
Hardy, Dudley
    Yellow Girl 11
Harfort 149
Harlow, Jean 72, 81, 90–92
Hart, William S. 132
Hassall, John 14
Haussmann, Raoul 40
Hay, Will 105, 108
Haycock Press, The 112
Hayworth, Rita 72, 89, 169
Hazan, Jack 214
Hazards of Helen, The 73
Heart Specialist, The 60, *63*
Heartfield, John 40
Heliotype 64
Hell's Angels 72, 90, *91*
Helm, Brigitte 33
Helpmann, Robert 108
Herzog, Werner 200, 201, 207
High Sierra 68
Hildebrandts
    Star Wars 217
Hirschfeld, Al
    New York, New York 216
    Sunshine Boys, The 216
Histoire d'un Crime* 132
Hitchcock, Alfred 73, 100
Hockney, David
    A Bigger Splash 214, 216
Hoffmann, Josef 10
Hohenstein, Alfred 10, 159
Holiday Inn 82
Holloway, Stanley 110, 111
Hound of the Baskervilles, The 217
Housing 193
Hughes, Howard 72, 91
Hurry, Leslie 108, 113
    Dead of Night 108, *113*

I Walked with a Zombie 68, *78*
Idiot's Delight 217
Ievstayev, Mikhail and Leonid Voronov
    October 52
Ikimono no kiroku 200, *210*
Il Vangelo Secondido Matteo 173, *190*
Ilyinsky, Igor 46, 47, 49
Im Lauf der Zeit 201, *205*
Impressionism 133
Incredible Shrinking Man, The 73, *96*
Invaders from Mars 73, *96*
It 72, *95*
It Happened in Brooklyn 68, *80*, 81

Jacoby, Georg 27
Jacquelin, Jean 149

Jailhouse Rock 217
Jakubowska, Wanda 159, 160
Jannings, Emil 27
Janowitz, Hans 26
Jara, Victor 196
Jeanne, Marcel 149
Joan the Woman 60, *66*, 67
Johnson, Lyndon B. 193
Joly-Normandin system 15, 21
Jorio, Albert 149
Judith of Bethulia 56, 63
Jugendstil 23
Julian, Rupert 65, 76

KADR 160
Kaiser, the Beast of Berlin 65, *76*
Kameradschaft 36
Karloff, Boris 64
Karussell des Lebens 27, *28*
Kauffer, E. McKnight 117
    Metropolis 117
Keaton, Buster 64, 69
Kelly, Gene 80, 81
Kennel Murder Case, The 68, *85*
Kestleman, Morris 108
    San Demetrio, London 105, 108
Keystone 56, 59
Kid, The 65, *76*
Kinetoscope 14
King Kong 64
King of the Wild 64, *75*
Kino-Eye principles 23, 33, 44, 45
Kino-Pravda 44
Kinopodotel 40
Kinski, Klaus 200, 207
Kirchner, Ernst Ludwig 23
Kleine, George 56
Klimt, Gustav 10
Kluge, Alexander 201
Kokoschka, Oskar 23
Komarov, Sergei 49
Korda, Alexander 96
Kozintsev, Grigori 45
Kracauer, Siegfried 36
Krauss, Werner 26, 27
Krupskaya, Nadezdha 40
Kubrick, Stanley 212, 213
Kuleshov, Lev 42, 49
Kurosawa, Akira 200, 203
Kuzmina, Elena 48, 49
Kyrle Picture Palace, Ross *15*

La Nouvelle Vague 145
Labisse, Felix 149
Lac des Cygnes, Le 107
Ladd, Alan 72, 88
Lady from Shanghai, The 72, *89*
Lady in the Dark 68, 82, *86*
Ladykillers, The 108
Laemmle, Carl 56, 60
Lake, Veronica 72, 88, 89
Lancaster, Osbert
    Laxdale Hall 111, *118*, 119
Lancy, Bernard 141, *150*, 151, 216
    Les Enfants du Paradis 141, *150*, 151
    La Grande Illusion 151
    Le Jour se Leve 151
    La Kermesse Heroique 151
    La Kermesse Rouge 148
Lang, Fritz 30, 33–35, 117, 133
Larionov, Mikhail 39, 45
Last Laugh, The 27
Lavinsky, Anton 49
    Battleship Potemkin 49, 52
Lawrence, Florence 56, 60
Le Roy, Mervyn 159
Lebenszeichen 201
Lee, Peter 112, 116
Lef 42, 44
Lefebvre, René 149
Leger, Fernand 133, *139*
Leni, Paul 36
Lenica, Jan 160, 169
    Marriage in the Dusk 160, *168*, 169
    We are all Murderers 160, *164*, 165
Lenin, Vladimir Ilyich 40
Leonidov, Leonid 46, 49
Leopard Man, The 68, *78*
Levet, P. 149
Levy, Charles 13, 15
Lewton, Val 68, 78
L'Herbier, Marcel 133
Libeled Lady 68, 72, *81*
Lissitsky, El 42, 200

Little Annie Rooney 64, *71*
Little Lord Fauntleroy 64, *70*
Lodz – the Polish Manchester 159
Lombers, Eric 118
London Film Productions 105
London Transport 111, 118
Lonsdale and Bartholomew 112
Lorant-Heilbron, V. 132
    La Grève 132
Lorre, Peter 68, 82
Lost World, The 61
Loves of Joanna Godden, The 108
Loy, Myrna 65, 77, 81
Lubitsch, Ernst 26–28, 36
Lucas, George 217
Lumière, Auguste 14, 17, 20
Lumière, Louis 14, 17, 20, 131
Lyon, Ben 60, 72

Maciste Contre Tous 132, *134*
Mackintosh, Charles Rennie 10
Madame Dubarry 27
Madaré 10
Makk, Karoly 165
Malclé, Jean-Denis 144
    La Belle et la Bête 144, *154*, 155
Malevich, Kazimir 39, 44
Mallet-Stevens, Robert 133
Maltese Falcon, The, 68, *85*, 217
Manet, Edouard 165
    Les Chats 10
Mankiewicz, Joseph L. 73, 103
Marchetti 15
Marczewski, Wojciech
    Nightmares 169, 185
Mariani 149
Marinetti, Tomasso 39
Marshall, Francis 128
Martinez, Raul 196
    Lucia *194*, 196
Marx Brothers 65, 75
Marx, Roger 10
Mascot 64
Mascii, Jean 149
Mason, James 108
Mataloni, G. M. 10, 159
Matejko, Theo 26
    Der Golem 26, 28, *29*
    Tartüff 27, *32*, 33
Mauzan, Achille Luciano 15
    Les Vampires 132
Mayakovsky, Vladimir 44
Mayer, Carl 26, 27, 33
Maze, The 73, *96*
Médecin malgré lui 15
Medley, Robert
    Bitter Springs 111, *120*
    Saraband for Dead Lovers 110, 111
Méliès, George 130, 131
Menzies, William Cameron 73, 96, 117
Mercier, Jean-Albert 133
    Les aventures de Robert Macaire 133
    Fantômas 133
    La Fin du Monde 133
    14 Juillet 137, *139*
    Mauprat 133
    Le Million 137
    A Nous la Liberté 137
    La Proie du vent 137
    Six et Demi-Onze 133
Mesnier, Paul 144
Metlicovitz, Leopoldo 10, 159
Metro-Goldwyn-Mayer 60, 61, 65, 72, 73, 78, 80, 81
Metropolis 30, 33, *34*, *35*, 117, 133
Michel, Karl
    Faust 24, *25*, 30
Mifune, Toshiro 200, 203
Mildred Pierce 217
Minter, Mary Miles 60, 63
Minton, John 114
    Eureka Stockade 111, *114*, 128
    Where no Vultures Fly 111
Moholy-Nagy, Lazlo 40, 200
Molière 15, 27, 33
Monogram 72, 96, 97
Monument to the III International 39
Monroe, Marilyn 72, 92, 93, 217
Moor, D.
    Have you volunteered? 40
Moreau, Jeanne 145, 185

Morgan Lithograph Company 60, 65, 68
Morocco 72, *94*, *95*
Morrow, Albert George 14
Morvan, Hervé 149
Moser, Koloman 10
Moskvin, Ivan 49
Mother 49
Motion Picture Patents Company 55, 56, 59
Mount, Reginald
    Train of Events *123*
Mozley, Charles 105
Mucha, Alphonse 10, 15
    Gismonda 10
Mucharski, Jan 159
Munch, Edvard 23, 26, 28
Munk, Andrzej 165, 176
Murnau, F.W. 25, 27, 30, 36
Mussolini, Benito 159, 169
Mysterious Mr Moto 68, *82*

Naruse, Mikio 200
Nasfeter, Janusz 165
National Screen Service 112
National Socialism 23, 36
Naumov, Aleksandr 40, 49
Nazimova, Alla 61, 65
Neame, Ronald 111
Negri, Pola 26–28
Neo-realism 36, 144, 159, 169, 173, 185, 186
Neue Sachlichkeit 33, 36
Niagara 72, 92, *93*
Nicholson, William 11
Nielsen, Asta 27, 30, 31
1905 42
Niven, David 111, 127
Noel, Guy-Gerard 149
Northbrooke, John 9
Notte, La 185
Nouvelle Mission de Judex, La 132
Novembergruppe 30, 42
Novy Lef 44

O'Brien, Willis 64, 67
Obmokhu 49
Offset printing 60, 68
Olivier, Laurence 105, 111
Orlov, Dmitry Stakhevich
    Have you volunteered? 40
Orazi, Manuel-Joseph Raphael 149
Ortazar, Octavio 196
Ossessione 169, 186, *187*
Otis Lithograph Company 65
Overlanders, The 111

Pabst, G.W. 30, 31, 33, 36, 37
Padron, Juan 196
Pagewood studios 120
Pagnol, Marcel 137
Paradise Canyon 72, 96, *97*
Paramount Pictures 60, 68, 72, 82, 112
Pasolini, Pier Paolo 173, 190
Passage to Marseille 68, *85*
Pathé, Charles 131, 132
Peacock Pie 121
Peak, Bob 218
    Apocalypse Now 213
    Excalibur 213
    In Like Flint 213
    Missouri Breaks 213, *218*
    Modesty Blaise 213
    Star Trek the Motion Picture 213
Pean, René 149
Pechstein, Max 30
Penfield, Edward 10, 11
Perez, Manuel 196
Perils of Pauline, The 64, 75
Peeping Tom 116, *125*
Peron, René 144, 148
    French Cancan 144, *153*
    Les Maudits 148
Pevsner, Antoine 40
Peynet, Raymond 149
Phantom of the Opera 65, *76*
Phono-Cinema-Theatre 15
Photo-montage 40, 42, 49, 200
Photogelatin 64
Photograms 200
Picasso, Pablo 39
Pick, Frank 111
Pickford, Mary 46, 47, 49, 63, 64, 70, 71
Pigeot, Pierre 149

Piper, John 108, 117
  The Bells go Down 108
  Painted Boats 108, *109*
  Pink String and Sealing Wax 108
Pipon Frères 14, 19
Poelzig, Hans 26
Poissonnié, Jean R. 137
  Les Bas-Fonds 137, *139*
Poitier, Sidney 73, 103
Polly 106
Pommer, Erich 26, 30, 36
Pop Art 171, 193, 196, 213
Poster sizes 60, 63
Postman Always Rings Twice, The 169
Powell, Michael 111, 116, 125, 127
Powell, William 65, 68, 77, 81, 85
Praxinoscope 12–14
Preminger, Otto 73, 98, 99, 101, 102
Presley, Elvis 217
Pressburger, Emeric 111, 125
Prévert, Jacques 141
Price, Dennis 108
Professor Beware 56, *63*
Projections Animées 14, *19*
Proletkino 40
Proletkult 40
Propagandastaffel 141
Protazanov, Yakov 44, 46, 49
Prusakov, Nikolai 40
  Bureaucrats and People 46, 47, 49
  Five Minutes that Shook the World 49
  Great Tragedy of a Small Woman 49
Pryde, James 11
Public Enemy, The 72, *92*
Pudovkin, Vsevolod 42, 49
Pulford, Eric 111, 112
  Breathless 112
  Cromwell 112
  The Evil that Men Do 112
  Gaslight 112
  The Golden Voyage of Sinbad 112
  Henry V 112
  The Horse's Mouth 111, *118*
  Khartoum 112
  Odd Man Out 112
  Oliver Twist 112
  Waterloo 112

Quatre Cent Coups, Les 145
Queen Elizabeth 60
Quo Vadis? 56, *63*, 64

Rabier, Benjamin 149
Radford, Basil 108
Raimu 137, 143
Rambova, Natasha 65, 76
Rand, Paul, 99
Rank Organization 112
Ray, Man 200
Raymundo
  Ukamau 196, *197*
Rayonnism 39
Reboira 196
Reed, Carol 111
Reed, Charles 112
Reinhardt, Max 26, 27
Reiss, Manfred
  Against the Wind 123
Reisz, Karel 116, 129
Reklam Film 40
Renoir, Jean 133, 137, 141–144, 156
Renoir, Pierre 137, 141
Republic 64, 72
Return of the Jedi 217
Revenge of the Jedi 217
Reynaud, Emile 12–14
Rice, Burton
  Woman 56, *57*, 65
Riccordi printing house 15
Richard III 104, 105, 111
Richardson, Tony 116, 129
Ringling Brothers Circus 13
Ripley 112
Riso Amaro 173
Ritchie, Alick P.F. 14
RKO Pictures 65, 68, 78
Roaring 20s, The 68, *87*
Roberty 149
Rocco e i Suoi Fratelli 173, 185

Rockwell, Norman
  The Magnificent Ambersons 72, *217*
  The Song of Bernadette 72
Rocky Mountain 68
Rodchenko, Alexander 39, 40, 42, 44
  Battleship Potemkin 41, 44
Roeg, Nicholas 218, 219
Rogers, Ginger 80, 82, 86
Rojac, Roger 149
Roma Citta Aperta 169
Rossellini, Roberto 169
ROSTA posters 49
Rostgaard, Alfredo 196
  Hanoi, Martes 13 193, 194, *195*
Rothholz, H.A.
  They Came to a City 108
Rotogravure 64
Rukhlevsky, Yakov 40
Rutherford, Margaret 111, 124
Ruttmann, Walther 22, 23, 33, 44
Rychkov, Grigory 40

Sachs, Kupfer
  Things to Come 119, 128
Saint Orphée martyr de la poesie et de la musique 144
Salomé 61, 65
Sanjines, Jorge 196
Saturday Night and Sunday Morning 116, *129*
Savignac, Raymond 149
Scarfe, Gerald 214
  The Wall 216
Scarlet Empress, The 72, *94*
Schufftan, Eugene 33
Schulz-Neudamm 33
  Metropolis 33, *34*
Schutz, Zsigo Eiben
  Things to Come 117
Scotson-Clark, F. 10, 11
Searle, Ronald 216
  Castle in the Air 111, *124*
  The Lavender Hill Mob 110, 111
  The Pure Hell of St Trinians 111, *124*, 125
Secessionists, The 10
Sedgwick, Edward 64
Sedgwick, Eileen 64
Semionov, Semion
  A Kiss for Mary Pickford 46, 47, 49
  Turksib 49, *51*
Senefelder, Alois 9
Serenander, Bengt 216
Serials 64, 75
Seven Year Itch, The 72, *92*
Shadow of the Thin Man 65, *77*
Shearer, Norma 217
Sherman Anti-trust Act, The 55
Shriek of Araby, The 64, *70*
Sickert/Noss
  Traumstadt 205
Silk screen 193, 196
Sim, Alastair 108
Simbari 112
Simenon, Georges 137
Simmons, Jean 163
Simon, Simone 137, 140
Sinatra, Frank 80, 98
Singin' in the Rain 68, 80, 81
Smith, Jack 213
Smoliak, Nikolai
  The Conveyor of Death 51
Smouldering Fires 65, *74*, 75
Socialist Realism 51, 52, 159, 160
Solas, Humberto 196
Son of the Sheik 65, *76*
Song of the Thin Man, The 65, *77*
Soubie, Roger 149
Sovkino 40
SSSR na Stroyka 44
Stafford 112
Stahl-Arpke, Otto
  Das Cabinet des Dr Caligari 24, 26
Stalin, Joseph 51, 52, 160
Starowieyski, Francisek 165, 185
  Coloured Stockings 165, *181*
  Everything for Sale 169, *183*
  Fanfare 165, *174*
  The First Race 165
  The Forty First 165, 174, *175*
  The House Under the Rocks 165, *181*
  Illumination 169, *184*, 185

La Loi des Rues 165, *181*
Mother 165
Nightmares 169, *184*, 185
The Ninth Circle 165, *182*, 183
Samson 165, 169, 178, *179*
St Peter's Umbrella 165, *174*
Stories not from this Earth 165, *181*
Le Trois Font la Paire 165, *178*
START 159, 160
Steadman, Ralph
  Almonds and Raisins 214, 216
Steamboat Bill Jr 64, *69*
Steinberg, Saul 213
Stenberg Brothers, The 33, 45
  Earth 50, 51
  Fragment of an Empire 42, *43*
  Katka's Reinette Apples 45, 46, 47
  The Man with the Movie Camera 38, 39, 52, *53*
Stobbs
  A Kid for Two Farthings 111, *118*
Stone lithography 60, 67, 68, 74, 82, 96, 97, 112, 132
Storm Over Asia 49
Strike 42
Strobridge Lithographic Company 13, 15
Sturges, Preston 72, 89
Sturm group 26
Sugata Sanshiro 200, *211*
Sulkari 197
Sullivan's Travels 72, *89*
Suprematism 40
Swedish Film Institute, The 216
Swierzy, Waldemar 165, 171
  The Law is the Law 165, *180*, 181
  Midnight Cowboy 165, *171*
  The Witches 165, *168*, 169
Syndicate of Film Poster Designers, The 137, 141, 151

Talmadge, Norma 56, 200
Tamagno 137
  Cinématographe and Phonographe 15
  Napoléon 133, 137
  Verdun Tel Que Poilus l'a Vecu . . . 133, *136*, 137
Taste of Honey, A 129
Tati, Jacques 144, 153
Tatlin, Vladimir 39, 44
Taxi! 68, *85*
Taylor, William Desmond 63
They Died with their Boots on 68, *84*
Third World Cinema 193
This Gun for Hire 72, *88*
This Land is Ours 193
Thompson, Bradbury 99
3-D 73
Time After Time 218
Tissé, Edouard 40
Toe, Andre 137
  Le Schpountz 137, *143*
Tolstoy, Leo 49
Tomaszewski, Henryk 159, 160, 166
  Battle of the Rails 160, *161*
  Black Narcissus 160, *163*
  Five from Barska Street 160, *172*, 173
Tooker Lithograph Company 68
Torrence, Ernest 64, 69
Toulouse-Lautrec, Henri de 10, 15
  Divan Japonais 10
Tourneur, Maurice 56, 57, 65
Towards the Dictatorship (of the Proletariat) 42
Trauberg, Leonid 45
Trepkowski, Tadeusz 159, 160
  The Last Stage 159
  My Universities 158, 159, 160
  Random Harvest 159
Trinder, Tommy 108
Trotsky, Leon 52
Truchet, Abel 14
True, William 14
Truffaut, François 144
Tschichold, Jan 200
  Die Kameliendame 200
Turin, Viktor 49
Turpin, Ben 64, 70
Twentieth Century Fox 68, 73, 82

Ukigumo 200, *210*
Under the Phrygian Star 160
Ungerer, Tomi 213
  Dr. Strangelove 212, 213
United Groups of Film Producers 160
Universal Pictures 64, 72
Universum Film Aktien Gesellschaft 26, 27, 33, 36

Valentino, Rudolph 56, 64, 70, 76
Vargas, Alberto
  Behave Yourself 89
  The Flame of New Orleans 89
  Moon Over Miami 72, *89*
  Suddenly it's Spring 89
Vega, Luis
  Caminos de lost Hombres 196, *197*
  Terror Ciego 198, *199*
Vendetta, la 199
Vérne, Jules 131
Vertov, Dziga 23, 33, 40, 44, 53
Victimes de l'Alcoolisme, Les 132
Vidor, King 60, 61
Vigo, Jean 137, 144
Vila, Emilio 132
  Tih Minh 132
Villemot, Bernard 149
Visconti, Luchino 169, 173, 186, 187
Visiteurs du Soir, Les 141, *148*
Vkhutemas 40, 49
Von Sternberg, Joseph 72, 94, 95
Voronov, Leonid and Mikhail Iesteyev
  October 52
Voyage dans la Lune, Le 131
Vrai Bandit, Un 132, 134, *135*

Wagner, Fritz Arno 36
Wajda, Andrzej 160, 169, 176, 179, 183
Walker, Frederick
  Woman in White 11
Warner Brothers 56, 59, 68, 200
Warhol, Andy 213
Waxman, Harry 127
Way Down East 60, *62*, 63
Wayne, John 72, 96, 97
We Have Always on Hand a Keystone Comedy 59
Weber
  Westfront 1918 36, *37*
Wedekind, Frank 36
Wegener, Paul 26
Welles, Orson 72, 77, 89, 217
Wenders, Wim 201
Wernerowa and Biernacka
  Brief Encounter 160, 162, *163*
West of Zanzibar 111
Whale, James 28
White, Pearl 64
Widmark, Richard 73, 103
Wiene, Robert 26
Wilde, Oscar 61
Wilder, Billy 73, 102
Wine of Youth, The 60, *61*
Winning of Barbara Worth, The 72
Wisdom, Norman 112
Withers, Googie 108
Withers, Jane 216
Wizard of Oz, The 217
Woman of Affairs, A 68, *78*
Woods, S John 105
  Champagne Charlie 108, *117*
  The Lavender Hill Mob 110, 111
  The Loneliness of the Long Distance Runner 116, *129*
  Passport to Pimlico 108
Woolrich, Cornell 145
Wright, Matvyn
  The Halfway House 108
Wysard, Tony 128

Yojimbo 200, 202, *203*

Zanussi, Krysztof 169, 184, 185
Zavattini, Cesare 169, 173
Zaza 68, *82*
Zecca, Ferdinand 132
Zhukov, Pyotr and Grigory Borisov
  The Living Corpse 47, 49